GOD SPEAKS TO MAN

CHRISTIAN FOUNDATIONS

A series edited by Philip E. Hughes

GOD SPEAKS TO MAN

REVELATION AND THE BIBLE

by

J. I. PACKER

THE WESTMINSTER PRESS
Philadelphia

LIBRARY OF CONGRESS CATALOG CARD No. 66-11607

Published by The Westminster Press
Philadelphia, Pennsylvania ®

PRINTED IN THE UNITED STATES OF AMERICA

CONTENTS

FOREWORD

CHRISTIAN FOUNDATIONS is a series of paperback books written
by evangelical churchmen and designed to reaffirm the doctrine of the New Testament in the light of the past history,
the present needs, and the future development of the Church.
The series appears under the auspices of the Evangelical Fellowship in the Anglican Communion, and the authors are all
members of that Communion. But their concern is for the
whole Church, and not for just one portion of it. They have no
desire to promote any kind of narrow denominationalism or to
avoid involvement in the contemporary ecumenical debate.
As the Archbishop of Sydney said in his Foreword to the
British edition, 'These books have a truly catholic scope, and
accordingly they can speak with clarity and also charity to
those on either side of Anglicanism, and indeed, to many who
at present are outside the fellowship of Christian believers'.
The unity that the authors covet for the Church is unity in the
truth—not unity at any price, least of all at the price of dispens-
ing with the foundations of the faith which has been once de-
livered to the Church. They are convinced that, as evangelicals, they have a full and essential contribution to make, especially in advocating the recovery of the dynamic witness, the
apostolic teaching, the fellowship in worship, and the victorious
living of the New Testament; for these, they believe, are the
vital principles of Christian unity in faith and action.

In view of the fact that some of the books deal with con-
troversial issues, it is not expected that there will always be
agreement with each particular position that may be pro-
pounded; but it is hoped that the books will be received in the
spirit in which they are offered, which is not one of contention
but of goodwill and reasonableness. The authors only ask for
an unprejudiced hearing. Naturally they seek to persuade; yet
where they fail to do that, they will be content if any discussion
that arises is conducted before the bar of the scriptural revelation. They wish that all together, however different their
viewpoints, might follow the example of the Christians in

7

Beroea who searched the Scriptures to see whether the things they had been told were true (Acts 17:10f.). To do just this could in itself hardly fail to have the effect of bringing us all closer together.

The central importance of the Bible in the history of the Christian Church scarcely stands in need of proof. It is shown, in the first place, by the attitude of Christ and His apostles to the Scriptures of the Old Testament and, in the subsequent centuries, by the Church's acknowledgement of the authenticity and authority of those writings which constitute the Canon (standard or norm by which all else must be judged) of the New Testament. Not until modern times has it become customary to question or deny that the Bible is the Word of God and therefore supremely binding on all and sundry in what it teaches. To treat the authority of Scripture, as so much contemporary theology treats it, as merely relative and subjective, and not as objective and absolute, can quite definitely not be described as either catholic or apostolic. In the pages that follow Dr. Packer describes the baneful effects of the humanistic approach to the Bible and makes a plea for a return to the classical view of Scripture as the dynamic and vitally existential Word of God, addressed to mankind, and demanding both our attention and our response of obedience and trust. He reminds us, too, that this response is itself the work of God the Holy Spirit, who not only assures us inwardly that the Bible is indeed the Word of God but also by this means leads us to the experience of a Christianity that is genuine and full of power.

P. E. H.

Note: In this book and in others of the CHRISTIAN FOUNDATIONS series, mention of the 'Articles' in general, or of certain 'Articles' in particular (for example, 'Article XI' or 'Article XXXVII') should be understood to refer to the Thirty-Nine Articles of Religion of the Church of England (1563). Parallels to many of the statements in these doctrinal formulae could have been cited, of course, from sixteenth-century Reformation confessions such as the Augsburg Confession (1530), the Second Helvetic Confession (1566), and the Scottish Confession (1560), and from later statements such as the Westminster Confession (1647).

CHAPTER ONE

THE LOST WORD

'Behold, the days come, saith the Lord God, that I will send a famine in the land, not a famine of bread, nor a thirst for water, but of hearing the words of the Lord. And they shall run from sea to sea, and from the north even to the east; they shall run to and fro to seek the word of the Lord, and shall not find it' (Amos 8 : 11f.).

Eight centuries before Christ, the northern kingdom of Israel was in confident mood. True, moral standards had crashed, little honesty was left in business, poor people were badly treated, and upper-class debauchery was a byword; but there was a trade boom on, money was flowing into the country, and society as a whole was affluent ('we never had it so good'). How could anyone be worried in such prosperity? Also, Israel had a national faith. Figures for church attendance were high. Public worship, with rich ritual and fine music, was a recognized part of community life (though congregations had publicly stated that they would not stand for sermons! – see Amos 2 : 12). Living on the capital of a great religious heritage, Israel did not doubt that God was on her side and would see her through all that the future might bring.

Into this complacent community God dropped a bombshell, in the shape of farmer Amos. Amos came storming into Samaria as a prophet of doom for Church and nation. God, he said, was about to judge His people (2 : 6–4 : 3). The wheel of retribution was already spinning, and would soon go faster. Recent disasters – the drought, the bad harvest, the famine, the epidemic, the earthquake – had shown God's displeasure clearly enough (4 : 6–11), and these were only a beginning; soon the whole nation would be enslaved and deported (5 : 27). (This happened fifty years later, under the Assyrians: see II Ki. 17.) Worse still, the streams of revelation were going to dry up. There would be 'a famine of hearing the words of the Lord'.

To appreciate what this meant, we must remember that Israel, as the covenant people of God, had been promised guidance by divine revelation whenever it was needed. Besides giving Israel His law, and charging the priests to teach it (Deut. 31 : 9ff.; cf. Neh. 8 : 1ff.; Hag. 2 : 11f.; Mal. 2.7f.), God had undertaken to send a succession of prophets, men with His Word in their mouths, who could give direction in times of personal and national perplexity. This was the immediate meaning of Moses' statement in Deut. 18.15, 'The Lord thy God will raise up unto thee a prophet from the midst of thee, of thy brethren, like unto me' (cf. verse 18). In the passage from which these words come, Moses forbids the Israelites to take up with sorcery, spiritism, or any of the other occult practices to which the Canaanites turned for day-to-day guidance (verses 9ff.). To do so, he says, will be both ungodly and unnecessary, since God himself through His messengers will supply all the guidance they need. Down the centuries, God had fulfilled this promise by giving Israel both great individual prophets who brought oracles for the whole nation (men like Amos himself) and also a host of lesser figures, 'seers' or cult-prophets, who gave oracles of guidance to individuals on consultation (for examples of this ministry, see I Sam. 9 : 6ff.; I Ki. 14 : 1ff., 22 : 5ff., II Ki. 8 : 8ff.; and Num. 22–24). But now, Amos declared, God purposed as an act of judgment to bring this whole prophetic ministry to an end. Prophecy would fail (and perhaps the teaching of the law too: cf. Ezek. 7 : 26). Those who would not listen to prophets when God sent them (Amos 2 : 11f.) would find that there were now no prophets to listen to (cf. Mic. 3 : 5–7; Lam. 2 : 9; Ps. 74 : 9). However much men might desire a word of guidance or assurance from God, they would not be able to find one. Amos pictured the scene of spiritual destitution that would result: restless, frantic souls wandering distractedly round the country, listening to all that was being said in hope of hearing God's voice, and listening in vain. Their hearts would be hungry, and their hunger would go unsatisfied. For them, the Word of God would be truly *lost*.

THE LEGACY OF LIBERALISM

Amos is a prophet for today. His words show us the present state of much of Christendom. His vision of spiritual starvation in Israel pictures ours: the famine with which he foresaw that God would judge His people is the present experience of a great part of the world Church.

Now this is an entirely unnatural state of affairs. The New Testament represents the Church as inheriting through Christ all God's promises of spiritual life and welfare (see II Cor. 1:20; Rom. 15:8ff.; Gal. 3:16ff., 31; and cf. Rom. 4:16–23; Heb. 6:12–20; 10:15–23, 13:5f.). The Church, therefore, has the promise of constant instruction, assurance, and guidance from God, just as Old Testament Israel had. Not, indeed, that the Church is promised a perpetual succession of prophets speaking by immediate inspiration, as in Old Testament times; instead, the Holy Spirit, 'who spake by the prophets', is given to abide with the Church and to interpret, authenticate, and apply Old Testament and apostolic teaching to each Christian generation (see Jn. 14:16, 16:7–14 with 6:45; I Cor. 2:4f. with verses 9–16; II Cor. 3:12–4:6; I Thess. 1:5, 2:13, 4:9; Heb. 3:7 ff.; I Jn. 2.20–27). This is how the promise of divine instruction is to find its fulfilment in the Christian era. In the light of this, we would expect to find the Church of every age, including our own, firmly convinced that the prophetic and apostolic witness of the two Testaments is the Word of God; clear as to its central message concerning God in Christ; and able to see plainly how this message impinges on men, with its demand for conversion and a life of faith, hope, love and obedience. To the extent to which clarity on these matters is lacking, we are forced to conclude that the Church is unhealthy and out of sorts.

What, then, must be said of the mass of our churches today? For at no time, perhaps, since the Reformation have Protestant Christians as a body been so unsure, tentative and confused as to what they should believe and do. Certainty about the great issues of Christian faith and conduct is lacking all along the line. The outside observer sees us as staggering on from gimmick to gimmick and stunt to stunt like so many drunks in a fog, not knowing at all where we are or which way we should be going. Preaching is hazy; heads are muddled; hearts fret; doubts drain our strength; uncertainty paralyses action. We know the Victorian shibboleth that to travel hopefully is better than to arrive, and it leaves us cold. Ecclesiastics of a certain type tell us that the wish to be certain is mere weakness of the flesh, a sign of spiritual immaturity, but we do not find ourselves able to believe them. We know in our bones that we were made for certainty, and we cannot be happy without it. Yet, unlike the first Christians who in three centuries won the

11

Roman world, and those later Christians who pioneered the Reformation, and the Puritan awakening, and the Evangelical revival, and the great missionary movement of the last century, we lack certainty. Why is this? We blame the external pressures of modern secularism, but this is like Eve blaming the serpent. The real trouble is not in our circumstances, but in ourselves. The truth is that we have grieved the Spirit, and God has withheld the Spirit. We stand under divine judgment. For two generations our churches have suffered from a famine of hearing the words of the Lord. For us, too, the Word of God is in a real sense *lost*.

A WRONG TURNING IN BIBLICAL CRITICISM

Why is this? For it is not as if the Bible were no longer read and studied in the churches. It is read and studied a great deal; but the trouble is that we no longer know what to make of it. Mesmerized by the problems of rationalistic criticism, we can no longer hear the Bible as the Word of God. Liberal theology, in its pride, has long insisted that we are wiser than our fathers about the Bible, and must not read it as they did, but must base our approach to it on the 'assured results' of criticism, making due allowance for the human imperfections and errors of its authors. This insistence has a threefold effect. It produces a new papalism – the infallibility of the scholars, from whom we learn what the 'assured results' are. It raises a doubt about every single biblical passage, as to whether it truly embodies revelation or not. And it destroys the reverent, receptive, self-distrusting attitude of approach to the Bible, without which it cannot be known to be 'God's Word written' (Article XX). The result? The spiritual famine of which Amos spoke. God judges our pride by leaving us to the barrenness, hunger, and discontent which flow from our self-induced inability to hear His Word.

The situation is as paradoxical as it is pathetic, for critical scholarship has always claimed that its microscopic historical analysis of the books of Scripture gives the Church the Bible in a way in which the Church never had the Bible before, and in one sense this is perfectly true. Critical scholarship has sharpened the tools of biblical exposition and clarified the meaning of many biblical passages. It has given us commentaries of the highest value. It has invented a technique of analysing Scripture thematically without which the theological dictionaries and biblical theologies of the past sixty years could never have been written. In these respects it has paid rich dividends. It would be a sin against light to deny this. The 1958 Lambeth Conference was right to record 'our debt to the host of devoted scholars who . . . have enriched and deepened our understanding of the Bible'.[1] Yet the constant complaint against critical scholarship from its inception has been that it takes away the Bible from the faithful – the opposite of what it intends. And this complaint is true also. Here lies the paradox of the critical movement: that it has given the Church the Bible in a way that has deprived the Church of the Bible, and led to a famine of hearing the words of the Lord.

What went wrong, we ask, to produce such an effect? Why, this. From the start, biblical criticism drove a wedge between revelation (the Word of God) and the Bible (man's written witness to the Word of God). It viewed the Bible as a library of human documents, fallible and often fallacious, and defended this as the only 'scientific' view. While allowing that the Word of God in history was the writers' theme, and that their writings do in some fashion mediate that Word, it refused to identify the writings with the Word. God's Word was one thing, Holy Scripture was another. By taking this line, the critical movement broke with the historic Christian understanding of the nature of Scripture, crystallized by Augustine when he put into God's mouth the words: 'Indeed, O man, what My Scripture says, I say.'[2] Treating this view, not as a mystery of the faith, but as a mere ignorant mistake, critical scholarship committed itself to a method of study which assumed that Scripture might err anywhere. It told the Church that the Bible could never be rightly understood till belief in its inerrancy was given up. It prescribed a new agenda for theology – not just to integrate and apply the biblical account of things, but also to check and correct it; and it condemned as unscientific all types of theology that did not accept this programme. Even today, its spokesmen remain convinced that those who hold the Bible to be inerrant cannot really understand it, and they still wage war against the classical Christian view of inspiration. Thus, by insisting that the Scriptures are not a fully trustworthy word

[1] *The Lambeth Conference 1958* (London, 1958), I, 33
[2] *Confessions*, xiii. 29.

13

from God, biblical criticism has taken from the Church the Bible that once it had.

It is as well to say at once where, at bottom, this approach seems to go astray. Its mistake is to ignore the fact that Jesus and His Apostles taught a definite doctrine of the nature of Scripture, a doctrine just as integral to their message as were their beliefs about the character of God. This doctrine appears in such statements as 'the scripture cannot be broken' (Jn. 10:35); 'it is easier for heaven and earth to pass away, than for one tittle of the law to fall' (Lk. 16:17); 'all scripture is inspired by God' (II Tim. 3:16, R.S.V.); and it appears also in the designation of the Old Testament as 'the oracles of God' (Rom. 3:2; cf. Acts 7:38). It is further manifested whenever Christ and his apostles cite an Old Testament text to settle a point and clinch an argument, or quote an Old Testament statement, not ascribed to God in its context, as an utterance of God spoken through human lips. Examples are, 'he which made them . . . said . . .', Mt. 19:4, citing Gen. 2:24; 'O Lord . . . who by the Holy Ghost, by the mouth of our father David thy servant, didst say . . .', Acts 4:24, citing Ps. 2:1f.; cf. Acts 1:16; '(he that) raised him from the dead . . . saith also in another psalm . . .', Acts 13:34, citing Ps. 16:10; 'well spake the Holy Ghost by Isaiah . . .', Acts 28:25, citing Is. 6:9f.; 'of the Son he (God) saith . . .', Heb. 1:8ff., citing Pss. 45:6f., 102:25ff.; 'the Holy Ghost saith . . .', Heb. 3:7, citing Ps. 95:7ff.; 'the Holy Ghost also beareth witness to us . . .', Heb. 10:16f., citing Jer. 31:33. Indeed, this doctrine of Scripture underlies the whole New Testament, gospels, Acts, epistles, and Revelation alike, inasmuch as they all represent the Christian dispensation of grace through Christ as God's fulfilment of His predictions made in the Old Testament. The conception of Scripture as a transcript of divine speech is just as basic to (say) the epistles to the Romans and the Hebrews as belief in divine providence is to the narrative of Acts, or belief in the Church's real union with Christ is to the argument of Ephesians. Belief that (to echo Augustine) God says what the Scriptures say is in truth the foundation-stone of all New Testament theology.

That being so, the issue between the modern critical movement and the older approach reduces to this: are the New Testament writers trustworthy teachers? and was the Lord Jesus Christ a trustworthy teacher? What grounds are there

14

for accepting the New Testament account of any act of God in this world, if we reject its account of His act of inspiring the Bible? If, on dominical and apostolic authority, we believe that God made His Son man, and redeemed us through the Cross, and regenerates believers by uniting them to the risen Christ, how can we withhold belief when the same authorities tell us that God so inspired the biblical writers that their word is also His Word? The grounds for accepting the instruction of Christ and His apostles on this point are the same as they are for accepting it on any other. The very reasons which we have for believing what they teach about sin, salvation, and the Church, forbid us to disbelieve what they teach about the Bible. Certainly, the fact of biblical inspiration cannot be verified by independent inquiry, but then neither can such facts as forgiveness or adoption. We believe in these things, not because we can prove them 'scientifically', but because we are assured of them by Christ and His apostles, whom we regard as teachers worthy of our trust. But we must not pursue these thoughts at present.

NEW VIEWS OF REVELATION AND INSPIRATION

A further fact heightens the paradox of our present situation. The era of biblical criticism has been marked, not only by intense study of the biblical text, but also by an unprecedented interest in the subjects of revelation and inspiration. Never in Christian history have these themes received so much concentrated attention as in the past hundred years. Never has the relevant biblical material been examined so thoroughly. And yet, for all this, the Word of God has been lost. Again we ask, what has gone wrong? Why has all this elaborate discussion, intended as it was to make the Word of God more plain and accessible to us, actually had a contrary effect? The answer is as before. The weakness of these theological discussions, as of the biblical studies that went with them, was that they drove a wedge between the living God in His revelation and the written word of the Bible.

Up to the nineteenth century, Protestant theology was accustomed to bracket revelation and inspiration together, subsuming the former under the latter. Revelation in the passive sense, meaning 'that which is revealed', was equated with the teaching of Holy Scripture, and God's revelatory action was discussed almost entirely in connection with the inspiring of the Bible.

15

Revelation, it was said, was the process whereby God disclosed to chosen men things otherwise unknowable (a definition based on Dan. 2 : 22, 28ff., 47, 10 : 1; I Cor. 2 : 9f.; Eph. 3 : 4f.; Rev. 1 : 1f.), and inspiration was the correlative process whereby He kept them from error when communicating, *viva voce* or in writing, that which He had shown them. A typical statement of this position is given by Charles Hodge in his *Systematic Theology* (1873). Referring to I Cor. 2 : 7–13 ('the wisdom that hath been hidden . . . things . . . which entered not into the heart of man . . . unto us God revealed them through the Spirit . . . which things also we speak . . . in words . . . which the Spirit teacheth'), Hodge writes: 'There is neither in the Bible nor in the writings of men, a simpler or clearer statement of the doctrines of revelation and inspiration. Revelation is the act of communicating divine knowledge by the Spirit to the mind. Inspiration is the act of the same Spirit, controlling those who make the truth known to others. The thoughts, the truths made known, and the words in which they are recorded, are declared to be equally from the Spirit. This, from first to last, has been the doctrine of the Church . . .'[1]

In the discussions of revelation and inspiration that went on under critical auspices, however, this neat correlation was given up. Also, the centre of interest shifted. Instead of being a mere preamble to the doctrine of inspiration, revelation now became a subject for study in its own right. It was seen that the biblical idea of revelation includes more than the older theology dealt with under this head. Revelation means the whole work of God making Himself known to men; the theme embraces, on the one hand, all the words and deeds of God in which the biblical writers recognized His self-disclosure, and, on the other hand, all that is involved in the encounter through which God brings successive generations to know Him through knowledge of the biblical facts. The Bible is thus the link between the revelatory events of the past and the knowledge of God in the present. Inspiration, therefore, should be studied as a sub-section of the doctrine of revelation, rather than vice versa. Inspiration is one of a long series of steps that God has taken to make Himself known to us, and ought to be treated as such.

This enlarging of the idea of revelation, and the dovetailing of inspiration into it, seems biblical and right. Less welcome, however, is the shrinking of the concept of inspiration that has

[1] C. Hodge: op. cit. (London, 1873), Vol. I, p. 162.

accompanied it. The belief that denials of the detailed truth of Scripture, made in the name of natural and historical science, were unanswerable, and, in particular, that Wellhausen's theory of pentateuchal origins, which dismissed much of the first five books of the Bible as non-Mosaic and non-factual, had to be accepted (as it still is in most text-books on the Old Testament),[1] led to reduced accounts of inspiration. According to these, inspiration was an enlightening of the biblical authors which, while it gave them moral and spiritual insight, and made their work 'inspiring' (or, as some say, a vehicle of God's Word to their readers), did not guarantee theological or historical trustworthiness to all that they actually wrote. Such accounts of inspiration are now largely standard in Protestant circles.

Hence, unlike their predecessors, modern Protestant theologians regularly insist that revelation and Scripture are two distinct things, and that to think of Scripture as written revelation is more misleading than helpful. Towards the close of *The Idea of Revelation in Recent Thought* (1956), John Baillie wrote: 'Each of the recent writers whom we have cited has been concerned to warn us against any simple identification of the Christian revelation with the contents of the Bible, and each has been well aware that in this respect he was breaking with a long-standing tradition.'[2] Once the idea of inspiration is weakened in the way described, this break is inevitable: we cannot identify the misconceptions of men with the Word of God. But now come the questions: if the relation between Scripture and revelation is not one of identity, what is it? And

[1] Wellhausen's theory has been damagingly criticized by conservative scholars such as W. H. Green: *The Higher Criticism of the Pentateuch* (New York, 1895); J. Orr: *The Problem of the Old Testament* (London, 1900); R. D. Wilson: *A Scientific Investigation of the Old Testament* (New York, 1926); O. T. Allis: *The Five Books of Moses* (Philadelphia, 1943); G. Ch. Aalders: *A Short Introduction to the Pentateuch* (London, 1949); E. J. Young: *Introduction to the Old Testament* (Grand Rapids, 1949; London, 1954). Roman scholars generally reject it, as does the modern Scandinavian school, but it keeps the field in most Protestant circles because no alternative theory seems to account for so many of the phenomena so neatly. It is admitted, however, by most scholars today that its truth is an open question, not a closed one, as was once thought. See *The New Bible Dictionary*, ed. J. D. Douglas, F. F. Bruce, J. I. Packer, R. V. G. Tasker, D. J. Wiseman (London, 1962), s.v. 'Pentateuch'.

[2] J. Baillie: op. cit. (London, 1956), p. 109.

how, in detail, are we to distil God's revelation from the total contents of the Bible? It is easy to say that Scripture 'inspires', and 'mediates the word of God', but what is the cash-value of such formulae when we have constantly to allow for undetectable possibilities of error on the part of each biblical author? These problems constitute a blank wall at which many present-day Protestants are staring. Much writing is addressed to them, but no agreed or even coherent solution has appeared so far; nor, perhaps, is one likely to. Meanwhile, uncertainty about the Bible pervades our churches, and we suffer from a famine of hearing the words of the Lord.

THE ENFEEBLING OF THE CHURCHES

The loss of the historic conviction that what Scripture says, God says, has weakened Protestant church life in this century in a number of ways.

First, it has *undermined preaching*. The true idea of preaching is that the preacher should become a mouthpiece for his text, opening it up and applying it as a word from God to his hearers, talking only in order that the text itself may speak and be heard, making each point from his text in such a manner 'that the hearers may discern how God teacheth it from thence' (Westminster Directory, 1645). But where there is doubt as to whether the texts of Scripture are words of God, preaching in this sense is impossible. All one can do then is purvey from the pulpit either 'church teaching', or else one's own private opinions. It is no wonder that the great evangelical preaching tradition of past days has almost petered out, and that many today have lost confidence in preaching as a means of grace.

Secondly, loss of conviction about the divine truth of the Bible has *undercut teaching*. Clergy are not sure what to inculcate as Christian truth; layfolk doubt whether what is taught in the Bible is worth learning. A spirit of unconcern about doctrine is abroad, a feeling that, since on so many issues it is anyone's guess what is true, it cannot much matter whether one has an opinion about them or not. Some clergy have ceased to try to teach the faith; many loyal church folk would not dream of trying to learn it. No wonder that a steady trickle of Anglicans, seeking certainty, turn to the Church of Rome or the cults.

Thirdly, uncertainty as to whether Bible teaching is God's

truth has *weakened faith*. St. Paul is insistent that religious devotion pleases God only so far as it expresses faith; otherwise it is mere unacceptable superstition (see Acts 17:22f., 30; Rom. 14:23). But faith, according to Paul, means the subjecting of mind and conscience to the Word of God, recognized as such (see Rom. 10:17; I Cor. 2:1–5; I Thess. 2:13). In the absence of certainty as to just what the Word of God is, superstition prevails, and instead of faith there is fog. Professed Christians, though earnest and sincere, then become like the Jews who had 'zeal for God, but not according to knowledge' (Rom. 10:2). Much devotion in churches today is hazy, anxious, and joyless, simply because people have not been taught, or do not dare, to slot their faith into Holy Scripture and venture their lives upon its 'precious and exceeding great promises' (II Pet. 1:4) as the sure words of a faithful Creator. Doubts and uncertainties about God and our standing with Him are poor companions to live and die with; but many today are never out of their company, because they know of no assurances from God on which their faith may rest. No wonder that the tide of faith ebbs, and that church people as a body are in low spirits, suffering from apathy and lassitude.

Fourthly, perplexities about Holy Scripture have *discouraged lay Bible reading*. The idea has spread that the Bible is a book full of pitfalls which only the learned can hope to avoid, that you cannot in any case trust it all, even when you have found out its meaning, and that it is really too hard a book for ordinary Christians to study with profit. Here, at least (some feel), the Reformers, with their insistence on the clarity of Scripture, were wrong, and the Romanists right! Well-meant popular books, rewriting the biblical message in the light of 'the assured results of criticism', deepen rather than dispel this impression. 'It is perhaps a pity,' wrote Professor D. E. Nineham recently, 'that the proposed new Anglican catechism appears to regard the private reading of the Bible as mandatory for every literate member of the Church. Is that realistic. . .?'[1] Many would echo Professor Nineham's doubt. No wonder the Bible is not much studied by the average churchman.

We have grown so used to this state of affairs that we tend to regard it as natural and normal. Sometimes, indeed, we

[1] D. E. Nineham: *The Church's Use of the Bible Past and Present* (London, 1963), p. 162.

represent it as a state of virtue (as is man's way with his weaknesses), censuring our predecessors for being too definite and dogmatic, and complimenting ourselves on being open-minded, flexible, and free from obscurantism. We must, however, be careful here. It has been well said that if you open your mind wide enough a great deal of rubbish will be tipped into it. The flexibility of those who are 'tossed to and fro and carried about with every wind of doctrine' (Eph. 4 : 14), 'ever learning, and never able to come to the knowledge of the truth' (II Tim. 3 : 7) is not commended by the apostle. Obscurantism – shutting one's eyes to God's facts – is always of the devil, and it would certainly be sin if, in the name of loyalty to Scripture, we closed our eyes to (not theories, but) facts found by history and science[1]; but we cannot regard ourselves as free from obscurantism if, out of supposed deference to history and science, we decline to face the fact that New Testament faith is marked by dogmatism throughout, and that this dogmatism is rooted in the conviction that the words of the Old Testament writers, and of Christ and His apostles, were words from God. Generally, however, modern Protestant theology does not reckon with this fact; hence it breathes a spirit very different from that of the New Testament. Self-styled radicals tell us that to put new life into us we need a wholly new theology, one that sits looser to biblical modes of thought than any before, in which our twentieth-century Christian consciousness may find its full expression. But if what we have said is right, our twentieth-century Christian consciousness is already far astray, and the course proposed would only lead us deeper into scepticism and spiritual barrenness. It is vain to push on along the wrong road. It would be disastrous to pin our hopes to ever more drastic applications of the false principle that theology is an exercise in religious self-expression. Some Anglicans, with desperate ingenuity, are already developing 'radical' theologies

[1] The accusation, often made, that evangelical (and, for that matter, Roman) biblical scholarship does just this is misguided. What it does, rather, is to face frankly the problems about the Bible which scientific and historical inquiry raises, and then to live with them until such time as satisfying solutions appear, on the principle, stated by Augustine, that 'if we cannot reconcile such a contradiction (sc., between the apparent results of secular study on the one hand and Bible study on the other) we are to suspend judgment, not doubting either the Holy Scripture or the results of human observation and reasoning, but believing that it is possible, given sufficient knowledge and understanding, to reconcile the apparent contradiction.'

20

of this kind, in hope of alleviating our spiritual destitution and evangelistic impotence. But the epitaph on such theologies would seem to have been spoken already by Amos: *'They shall run from sea to sea, and from the north even to the east; they shall run to and fro to seek the word of the Lord, and shall not find it.'* Our condition will never be eased till we humbly retrace our steps to the point where we first went wrong.

THE HISTORIC REFORMED POSITION

It will help us to do this if we now take note of what Reformed formularies teach about the Bible. Their position as a whole contrasts strikingly with that of many Protestants today. We shall quote most fully from the Thirty-Nine Articles, Homilies, and Book of Common Prayer of the Church of England, partly because these are the standards which the writer knows best, partly because the Homilies and Prayer Book show us principles about Scripture finding practical expression in worship and devotion, which is our special area of interest in this chapter. All the Reformed foundation-documents point in the same direction, and their teaching may for our purpose be summarized under the following three headings.

1. *The inspiration of Scripture as the Word of God.*

The Anglican formularies state that the ultimate author of Scripture is God Himself. The Bible is 'God's Word written' (Article XX), 'the very pure Word of God' (Preface, Concerning the Service of the Church). God 'caused all holy Scriptures to be written for our learning' (collect for Advent II; cf. 'God, who hast written thy holy Word for our learning': Visitation of the Sick). The Scriptures as a body were 'written by the inspiration of the Holy Ghost' and are thus 'the Word of the living God', 'his infallible Word' (an Information for them which take offence at certain places of the Holy Scripture: *The Homilies*).[1]

As such, the Scriptures are words of truth and wisdom: if we cannot see this, the fault is in us, the pupils, rather than in them, the text-book. 'It cannot . . . but be truth which proceedeth from the God of all truth; it cannot but be wisely and

[1] *The Homilies*, ed. G. E. Corrie (Cambridge, 1850), pp. 370, 378, 383.

21

prudently commanded, what almighty God hath devised, how vainly soever, through want of grace, we miserable wretches do imagine and judge of His most holy Word' (op. cit., p. 378). The Scriptures are wholly self-consistent, for the God of truth cannot contradict Himself; therefore 'it is not lawful for the Church to . . . so expound one place of Scripture, that it be repugnant to another' (Article XX). All that Scripture says, our formularies tell us, God Himself says. Biblical teaching is wholly divine. 'We are taught *by thy holy Word*, that the hearts of Kings are in thy rule' (holy communion; see Prov. 21:1). God is the One 'who *by thy holy Apostle* hast taught us to make prayers . . . for all men' (holy communion; see I Tim. 2:1). The precepts and commands of Scripture are treated throughout the Anglican formularies as abidingly valid expressions of God's will. So are its promises: note, as one example, the words from the prayer of St. Chrysostom, 'who . . . *dost promise* (the tense is a continuous present) that when two or three are gathered together in thy Name thou wilt grant their requests' (cf. Mt. 18:19f.). The gracious words which Scripture records Christ as having spoken when on earth are words which He speaks still : 'Hear what comfortable words our Saviour Christ (not said, but) *saith* . . .' (holy communion; compare 'our Saviour Christ *saith*' in the first prayer of the baptism service).

In the same vein, the Scots Confession of 1560 speaks of 'the written Word of God, that is, the Old and New Testaments, in those books which were originally reckoned canonical', and of 'the Spirit of God by whom the Scriptures were written' (XVIII), and affirms that in listening to the instruction of Scripture the Church 'hears . . . the voice of her own Spouse and Pastor' (XIX). So, too, the Second Helvetic Confession of 1566 declares that 'the canonical Scriptures of the holy prophets and apostles of both Testaments are the true Word of God', having intrinsic authority; 'for God Himself spake to the fathers, prophets, apostles, and still speaks to us through the Holy Scriptures' (I).

The ideas of biblical inspiration and authority which these statements reflect were drawn out more fully in the Westminster Confession of 1647. 'It pleased the Lord, at sundry times, and in divers manners, to reveal Himself, and to declare that His will unto His Church; and afterwards, for the better preserving and propagating of the truth . . . to commit the same wholly unto writing . . . The authority of the holy Scrip-

22

ture, for which it ought to be believed and obeyed, dependeth
... wholly upon God, (who is truth itself,) the author thereof;
and therefore it is to be received, because it is the Word of
God' (I.i, iv).

2. *The divine claim of Scripture as a rule of faith and life.*

Anglican formularies embody this claim both positively and
negatively, insisting that the way to serve God is by receiving
and following all that the Bible teaches, without either addition
or subtraction. They represent the service of God, in both
liturgy and life, as a matter of observing what 'the holy Scripture doth say' (marriage service) and doing throughout what
'the Scripture moveth us' (Morning and Evening Prayer) to do.
The supreme good which worshippers are taught to request
in the Litany is 'increase of grace, to hear meekly thy Word,
and to receive it with pure affection, and to bring forth the
fruits of the Spirit', 'the grace of thy Holy Spirit, to amend our
lives according to thy holy Word'. (Compare the similar request, that 'with meek heart and due reverence' we may 'hear
and receive thy holy Word', in the holy communion service.)
The supreme blessing sought for the newly-weds in the marriage service is that their life together may be ruled by the
Bible—'that whatsoever in thy holy Word they shall profitably learn, they may in deed fulfil the same'. The ideal for
all Christian people is to 'desire God's holy Scriptures; love
them; embrace them; so as at length we may be transformed
and changed into them' (*The Homilies*, p. 371), in the sense
that we may come to 'love the thing which thou commandest,
and desire that which thou dost promise' (collect for Easter
IV). The Scriptures are thus acknowledged to be, so to speak,
God's mould for shaping our whole lives.

The Articles develop the principle of biblical authority
polemically. Against Rome they affirm the sufficiency of Scripture. 'Holy Scripture containeth all things necessary to salvation; so that whatsoever is not read therein, nor may be proved
thereby, is not ... an article of the Faith, or ... necessary to
salvation' (Article VI). The first homily draws the moral: 'Let
us diligently search for the well of life in the books of the New
and Old Testament, and not run to the stinking puddles of
men's traditions ... for our justification and salvation' (*The
Homilies*, p. 2). Article XX states, also against Rome, the
further principle that the Church must subordinate itself to

Scripture in all its enactments. 'Although the Church be a witness and a keeper of holy Writ, yet, as it ought not to decree anything against the same, so besides the same ought it not to enforce anything to be believed for necessity of salvation.' All that the Church puts forward must be exposed to the critical judgment of Holy Scripture. The historic creeds are commended, because they pass this test (Article VIII); but not all the recorded decisions of general councils and particular churches do (Articles XXI, XIX); nor do such notions as works of supererogation (Article XIV), perfectionism (Article XV), salvation by sincerity (Article XVIII), purgatory, indulgences, image- and relic-worship, invoking the saints (Article XXII), worship in a foreign tongue (Article XXIV), and transubstantiation (Article XXVIII).

All private and traditional interpretations of Scripture must be scrutinized lest they misrepresent the detailed claims of Scripture by distorting its plain, natural sense, as determined from within. 'The infallible rule of interpretation of Scripture is the Scripture itself' (Westminster Confession, I.ix).

3. *Our dependence upon Scripture as a means of grace.*

The Anglican standards illustrate this point in great detail. They regularly speak of the written Word—read, preached, heard, applied—as the main channel of life from God to man. 'The Scripture of God is the heavenly meat of our souls; . . . it is a light lantern to our feet; it is a sure, steadfast, and everlasting instrument of salvation; . . . it comforteth, maketh glad, cheereth, and cherisheth our conscience . . . The words of Holy Scripture be called, words of *everlasting life*; for they be God's instrument, ordained for the same purpose. They have power to turn, through God's promise . . . and being received in a faithful heart, they have ever an heavenly spiritual working in them' (*The Homilies*, p. 3). Christ Himself, 'promising to be present with His Church till the world's end, doth perform His promise . . . in this, that He speaketh presently that is, here and now, unto us in the Holy Scriptures' (op. cit., pp. 370f.). Thus men are 'called by thy holy Word' to faith in Christ (collect for St. Andrew's Daye). Through the Word they are sanctified: when heard and 'grafted inwardly in our hearts', it will 'bring forth in us the fruit of good living' (holy communion). It is through 'comfort of the Scriptures' that God gives hard-pressed Christians hope (collect for Advent II), and bestows on the man 'troubled in mind or in conscience' 'a right

24

understanding of himself, and of thy threats and promises; that he may neither cast away his confidence in thee, nor place it anywhere but in thee' (Visitation of the Sick). In all these ways saving grace (that is, living and working faith) is mediated through the Scriptures. Therefore we pray for confirmation candidates that God will 'so lead them in the knowledge and obedience of thy Word, that in the end they may obtain everlasting life' (Order of Confirmation). And when deacons are made presbyters we ask that their preaching of the Word may be blessed to us – 'that we may have grace to hear and receive what they shall deliver out of thy most holy Word, or agreeable to the same, as the means of our salvation' (Ordering of Priests).

The formularies are concerned that the Word be *publicly read*: hence the Prayer Book lectionary, covering the Old Testament and Revelation once, and the rest of the New Testament twice, each year. Hence, too, the mass of Scripture woven into the set services. No form of worship in Christendom prescribes so much of the Bible for public use as does the Prayer Book.

The formularies are further concerned that the Word be *publicly preached*: hence the ordination charge to presbyters 'out of the same Scriptures to instruct the people', and 'to banish and drive away all erroneous and strange doctrines contrary to God's Word' (Ordering of Priests). Hence also the prayer in the Litany (and the very similar prayer in the holy communion service) that God will 'illuminate all Bishops, Priests, and Deacons, with true knowledge and understanding of thy Word; and that both by their preaching and living they may set it forth'. Hence, too, the question to candidates for the diaconate, 'Do you unfeignedly believe all the Canonical Scriptures?', and the charge to bishops, 'Think upon the things contained in this Book. Be diligent in them . . .' The Prayer Book reveals an overmastering desire that Anglican clergy should above all things be men of the Word.

Finally, the formularies are concerned that the Word be *privately studied*: not just by the clergy, but by all churchmen. 'Unto a Christian man, there can be nothing either more necessary or more profitable than the knowledge of Holy Scripture . . . as many as be desirous to enter into the right and perfect way unto God, must apply their minds to know Holy Scripture.' 'These books, therefore, ought to be much in our hands, in our eyes, in our ears, in our mouths, but most of all in our hearts.' 'There is nothing that so much strengtheneth our faith and trust in God, that so much keepeth up innocency and pureness of the heart, and also of outward godly life and conversation, as continual reading and recording [that is, recalling] of God's Word . . . on the other side, nothing more darkeneth Christ and the glory of God, nor bringeth in more blindness and all kinds of vices, than doth the ignorance of God's Word.' 'To be ignorant of the Scriptures is the cause of error . . . as St. Jerome saith, "Not to know the Scriptures is to be ignorant of Christ".' 'I say not nay, but a man may profit with only hearing; but he may much more prosper with both hearing and reading.' Therefore, 'let us night and day muse, and have meditation and contemplation in them. Let us ruminate and, as it were, chew the cud, that we may have the sweet juice, spiritual effect, marrow, honey, kernel, taste, comfort, and consolation of them . . . Let us pray to God, the only author of these heavenly studies, that we may speak, think, believe, live, and depart hence, according to the wholesome doctrine and verities of them. And, by that means, in this world we shall have God's defence, favour, and grace, with . . . peace and quietness of conscience; and . . . shall enjoy the endless bliss and glory of heaven' (*The Homilies*, pp. 1, 3, 4f., 372, 377, 379f.).

But is not the study of Scripture too bewildering and dangerous a business for laymen to engage in profitably? The first homily is at pains to insist that it is not. God is faithful, and will not let the humble go astray. 'I shall shew you how you may read it [the Bible] without danger or error. Read it humbly with a meek and a lowly heart, to the intent you may glorify God, and not yourself, with the knowledge of it: and read it not without daily praying to God, that He would direct your reading to good effect; and take it upon you to expound it no further than you can plainly understand it' (p. 6f.). The self-distrustful, prayerful Bible student will find that the meaning of the Word soon grows plain, one text interpreting another, through the illumination of 'the Holy Ghost, who inspireth the true meaning unto them that with humility and diligence do search therefor' (p. 8, quoting Chrysostom). The Bible is thus a book for all to 'read, mark, learn, and inwardly digest' (collect for Advent II), for their soul's health and as the means of their salvation.

There is a great and painful contrast between this rapt extolling of the Bible as our true light and chief means of grace and the casual, blasé, patronizing, superior attitude towards the Bible which is all too common today. Whereas the Reformers revered it, awestruck at the mystery of its divinity, hearing Christ and meeting God in their reading of it, we rather set ourselves above it, acting as if we already knew its contents inside out, and were indeed in a position to fault it as being neither wholly safe nor wholly sound as a guide to the ways of God. Both the spirit and the sentiment of the clergyman who in Convocation recently spoke of the Old Testament as containing 'spiritual junk' are unhappily typical of our age. Naturally, coming to Scripture in this frame of mind, we fail to gain a proper understanding of what it is all about. One of the many divine qualities of the Bible is this, that it does not yield its secrets to the irreverent and censorious. Down the ages the accusing voices of our Reformation formularies charge us to consider whence and how far we have fallen. They make us realize that through losing faith in the Bible we have also lost touch with God's law and Gospel, His commandments and His promises, and indeed with His Christ, who is the Christ of the Bible. (And what, after all, are the 'new theology' and 'new morality' of our day but exotic ways of advertising our ignorance of these things?) Our formularies teach us that our defection from the Bible is in truth a defection from the Gospel and from Christ Himself, and that this defection has brought us under judgment. The application which we have made of Amos 8:11f. is confirmed by the following passage from the homily entitled 'A Sermon, how dangerous a thing it is to fall from God':

'The displeasure of God towards us is commonly expressed in the Scripture by these two things: by shewing His fearful countenance upon us, and by turning His face or hiding it from us . . . by turning His face or hiding thereof is . . . signified . . . that He clearly forsaketh us, and giveth us over . . . when He *withdraws from us His Word, the right doctrine of Christ,* His gracious assistance and aid, which is ever joined to His Word, and *leaveth us to our own wit,* our own will and strength, He declareth then that He beginneth to forsake us . . .' (*The Homilies,* p. 81.)

The present state of our churches makes it hard to doubt that God has begun to forsake us in these days, as a judgment for our irreverent disregard of His written Word.

What are we to do? We cannot recall the Holy Spirit and revive God's work among us by our own action: to quicken us again is God's prerogative, and His alone. But we can at least take out of the way the stumbling-stones over which we have fallen. We can set ourselves to rethink the doctrines of revelation and inspiration in a way that, while not refusing the light which modern study has thrown on the human aspects of the Scriptures, cultural, linguistic, historical, and so forth, will eliminate its scepticism about their divinity and eternal truth. No task, surely, is more urgent. And this is the task which we shall attempt, at any rate in outline, in the following pages.

CHAPTER TWO

GOD'S WORD SPOKEN (I)

BASIC to the New Testament is the claim that Christianity is a revealed religion. The Greek word translated 'reveal' (*apokalypto*) means to unveil something that was previously hidden, or to bring into view something that before was out of sight. Christianity rests on an unveiling of the hidden Creator Himself; Christians enjoy 'the light of the knowledge of the glory of God in the face of Jesus Christ' (II Cor. 4:6). The process, whereby through His dealings with a single national family – Israel – God revealed Himself to men, reached its climax in the person, words, and works of Jesus of Nazareth, God's incarnate Son. So the Christian relevation-claim finds its final statement in the majestic opening words of the epistle to the Hebrews: 'God, having of old time spoken unto the fathers in the prophets by divers portions and in divers manners, hath at the end of these days spoken unto us in his Son' (Heb. 1:1f.). Of this revelatory process the sixty-six books of the Bible are both the product and the proclamation. The first thirty-nine (the Old Testament) span well over a thousand years of revelation to Israel; the last twenty-seven (the New Testament) were written in the second half of the first century. All these last have to do with God's crowning revelation in Jesus, who was crucified 'under Pontius Pilate' and raised from the dead, at some date between A.D. 26 and 36.

The opening words of Hebrews present the work of revelation as a divine activity ('*God* . . . hath . . . spoken') which in form was verbal ('God . . . hath . . . *spoken*') and cumulative ('in the *prophets* . . . in his *Son*'). In this and the next chapter we shall seek to open up the theme of revelation by exploring the significance of these three facts.

Revelation is a divine activity: not, therefore, a human achievement. Revelation is not the same thing as discovery, or the dawning of insight, or the emerging of a bright idea. Revelation does not mean man finding God, but God finding man, God sharing His secrets with us, God showing us Himself. In revelation, God is the agent as well as the object. It is not just that men speak about God, or for God; God speaks for Himself, and talks to us in person. The New Testament message is that in Christ God has spoken a word for the world, a word to which all men in all ages are summoned to listen and to respond.

To show what this means, we must here discuss three questions.

THE CHARACTER OF GOD

The first question is: Who is this God who has spoken? What sort of being is He?

The question is important, partly because misbelief about God's nature involves false views of revelation, partly because, according to the record, this is the basic thing that God's revelatory action was meant to make clear. God Himself was the supreme object of revelation from the start.

What, according to Scripture, has He revealed Himself to be?

First, He has shown Himself to be a *personal* being, one who calls Himself 'I' and speaks to man as 'you'. When, before the Exodus, He spoke to Moses at the burning bush, He gave His name as 'I am that I am' (perhaps more correctly, 'I will be what I will be': Ex. 3:14f., R. V. margin; cf. 6:2f.) – 'Yahweh' [Jehovah] for short. This name, like other God-given names (Abraham, Israel, Jesus, etc.), was a source of information about its bearer: it declared, on the one hand,

29

God's transcendent personality, His freedom and purposefulness, and, on the other hand, His self-sufficiency and omnipotence. The name 'Yahweh' is a standing witness against any notion of God as a mere impersonal principle: it declares that back of everything stands, not an aimless force – blind fate, or chance – but an almighty Person with a mind and will of His own.

When God brought His work of revelation to its climax by sending into the World His Son and His Spirit, He thereby showed Himself to be tri-personal – three Persons in one God. The Trinity is at the heart of the Christian revelation. Father, Son, and Holy Spirit' is God's New Testament 'name' (see Mt. 28:19) – in Karl Barth's happy phrase, His 'Christian name', expressing a basic truth about Him which only Christians know.

Second, God has shown Himself a *moral* being, One supremely concerned about right and wrong, whose dealings with men must be understood in moral terms, since they are determined by moral considerations. When at Sinai Moses asked to see God's glory, God proclaimed before him the following exposition of His 'name': 'The Lord, the Lord (Yahweh), a God full of compassion and gracious, slow to anger, and plenteous in mercy and truth; keeping mercy for thousands, forgiving iniquity and transgression and sin; and that will by no means clear the (impenitent) guilty: visiting the iniquity of the fathers upon the children . . .' (Ex. 34:6f.). God is perfect, not only in power, but also in love and purity, a God 'of infinite power, wisdom, and goodness' (Article I), 'a Spirit, infinite, eternal and unchangeable, in His being, wisdom, power, holiness, justice, goodness, and truth' (Westminster Shorter Catechism, Answer 4). God's own exposition of His name rules out all thought of Him as capricious, inconstant, untrustworthy, or unloving.

The impression is still abroad, despite many years of refutation, that the two Testaments represent God differently, the Old depicting Him as fierce in retribution, the New portraying Him as too merciful and mild to condemn anyone. But this is not so. The goodness and severity of God stand side by side in both Testaments. In the Old, the Holy God is unspeakably gracious to His people, as the Psalms constantly declare (cf. Pss. 92, 104, 105:1ff., 106:1f., 107, 108, etc.); while the New enlarges our view, not only of the glory of

30

God's mercy, but also – largely through Christ's own words (see Mt. 8:12, 10:28, 13:40ff., 25:41; Mk. 9:42–48; Lk. 13:1–5, 16:23–29, etc.) – of the terrors of God's judgment. In its picture of God, as in other things, 'the Old Testament is not contrary to the New' (Article VII), and the New, so far from cancelling the Old, merely endorses and amplifies it, thus fulfilling it. The God of both Testaments is one.

Third, God has revealed Himself to be the *source, stay, and end* of all creation, and of mankind in particular. 'Of him, and through him, and unto him, are all things' (Rom. 11:36). Paul develops these foundation-truths of theism in his sermon to the Athenian idolaters about the 'unknown God' (Acts 17:22ff.). First, he speaks of God as our *source*, the One who brought us into existence. 'The God that made the world and all things therein' (verse 24) 'created every race of men of one stock, to inhabit the whole earth's surface' (verse 26, *N.E.B.*). Then Paul speaks of God as our *stay*, the One who 'giveth to all life, and breath, and all things', so that 'in him we live, and move, and have our being' (verses 25, 28). We depend upon God every moment for our very existence: creatures only remain in being through the constant exercise of His upholding power (cf. Heb. 1:3). He, God transcendent, above and beyond and apart from His world, and entirely independent of it (cf. Acts 17:24f.), is also God immanent, in the world as the One who is over it, permeating and upholding it as the One who orders its goings and controls its course. Lastly, Paul speaks of God as our *end*. God made men, he says, 'that they should seek God' (verse 27). Man exists for God, and godlessness is a denial of man's own nature. Humanity is only perfected in those who know God. 'Man's chief end is to glorify God, and to enjoy him for ever' (Westminster Shorter Catechism, Answer 1).

This God, Paul adds, 'is not far from each one of us' (verse 27). Though He is 'Lord of heaven and earth' (verse 24), infinitely great, He is not remote. Just the opposite is true. The God who made the world is always, inescapably, our environment. Omniscient, omnipresent, unsleeping, undistracted, He is before and behind us, ever taking knowledge of us, whether or not we acknowledge Him. 'I the Lord search the heart, I try the reins . . .' (Jer. 17:10; cf. Ps. 139:1–5). We cannot hide from Him, even if we would; we live, willy-nilly, under His eye; and when He speaks it is our wisdom, no less than our duty, to heed what He says.

In view of the publicity given to the thesis of the Bishop of Woolwich that (as the title of his article in *The Observer* introducing *Honest to God* put it) 'our image of God must go', it is worth pointing out that this 'image' of God as personal, transcendent, immanent, holy, the source and goal of all things, is actually a *revealed description*. Any alternative 'image' of God, therefore, is false and idolatrous. In revelation, God tells us what He is like, and it is not for us to amend His testimony, as if we knew Him better than He knows Himself!

Certainly, the writer to the Hebrews thinks of the God who has spoken as corresponding to the description given above. God, to him, is the living Lord of the Old Testament (3:12, 10:31), the maker and upholder of all things (1:2, 11:3); a personal Being who talks to men (1:1, 11:7f., 12:25, 13:5), whose word searches the heart (4:12), and who knows us through and through (4:13); a God who keeps His promises (6:13–18); a just Judge (10:30, 12:23, 13:4), and a consuming fire against the defiant and contemptuous, who spurn the law and the Gospel (2:1–3, 6:6–8, 10:26–31, 12:29); a loving Father to His own people (12:5f.); a King whose throne is a throne of grace (4:16), and who rewards all who seek Him in faith (11:6, cf. verse 16). This, and none other, the writer tells us, is the God 'with whom we have to do' (4:13).

THE PURPOSE OF GOD

Our second question is: why has God spoken? He is self-sufficient, and does not need men's gifts or service (Acts 17:25); to what end, then, does He bother to speak to us?

The truly staggering answer which the Bible gives to this question is that God's purpose in revelation is to *make friends* with us. It was to this end that He created us rational beings, bearing His image, able to think and hear and speak and love; He wanted there to be genuine personal affection and friendship, two-sided, between Himself and us – a relation, not like that between a man and his dog, but like that of a father to his son, or a husband to his wife. Loving friendship between two persons has no ulterior motive; it is an end in itself. And

32

this is God's end in revelation. He speaks to us simply to fulfil the purpose for which we were made; that is, to bring into being a relationship in which He is a friend to us, and we to Him, He finding His joy in giving us gifts and we finding ours in giving Him thanks.

That God made man to be His friend appears from the third chapter of Genesis, where we find God walking in the garden in the cool of the day, looking for Adam to join Him and share His company (Gen. 3:8). That, despite sin, God still wants human friends appears from Christ's statement that God seeks true worshippers (Jn. 4:23); for *worship*, the acknowledging of *worth*, is an activity of friendship at its highest (hence 'with my body I thee *worship*' in the marriage service). God wants men to know the joy of the love-relationship from which worship springs, and of the worship itself in which that relationship finds its happiest expression. The supreme example of such a relationship with God is that of Abraham, who worshipped God and trusted and obeyed His word even to the point of being willing to surrender his son for sacrifice – and Abraham, we are told, 'was called *the friend of God*' (Jas. 2:23, alluding to Is. 41:8; cf. II Chr. 20:7). It is to make us His friends, as Abraham was, that God has spoken to us.

And if He was to succeed in making friends, it was absolutely necessary that He should speak to us; for the only way to make friends with a person is by talking to him and getting him to talk back to you. Friendship without conversation is a contradiction in terms. A man with whom I never speak will never be my friend. The thing is impossible.

Friendship is never fully enjoyed while the friends are out of each other's sight. Looks express affection better than mere words can, and the delight of a love-relationship can only be complete when we are looking into the beloved one's face. So, when someone we are fond of is away from us, we write, 'I'm longing to *see* you again.' The Bible looks on to a day when the relationship between God and His human friends will be made perfect in this way, a day when, in addition to hearing His voice, they will see His face. 'Now we see in a mirror, darkly; but then *face to face*' (I Cor. 13:12). Similarly, Scripture tells us that in the New Jerusalem those whom Jesus called 'friends' when He was on earth (see Jn. 15:13–15) 'shall *see his face*' (Rev. 22:4). Thus, dying Mr. Stand-fast, in Bunyan's *Pilgrim's Progress*, could confidently declare: 'I am going now to see that Head that was crowned with thorns, and that Face that was spit upon, for me. I have formerly lived by hear-say, and faith, but now I go where I shall live by sight, and shall be with him, in whose company I delight myself.' And by this vision both friendship and revelation will be perfected. But meanwhile God's friendship with men begins and grows through speech: His to us in revelation, and ours to Him in prayer and praise. Though I cannot see God, He and I can yet be personal friends, because in revelation He talks to me.

Some modern divines posit an antithesis between 'personal' and 'propositional' revelation, arguing that if revelation were propositional it would not be personal, and that since it is personal (God revealing Himself) it cannot be propositional (God talking about Himself). But this is absurd. Revelation is certainly more than the giving of theological information, but it is not and cannot be less. Personal friendship between God and man grows just as human friendships do – namely, through talking; and talking means making informative statements, and informative statements are propositions. To deny that revelation is propositional in order to emphasize its personal character is like trying to safeguard the truth that cricket is played with a bat by denying that it is played with a ball. The denial undercuts the assertion. To say that revelation is non-propositional is actually to *depersonalize* it. As Dr. F. I. Anderson says: 'To belittle propositions because they are impersonal is to destroy human relations by despising their normal medium. The bliss of being loved is different from the words of love-making, but the "proposition", "I love you", is a welcome, nay, indispensable means to the consummation of love in actuality. But in modern theology we have a Lover-God who makes no declarations!'[1] From which it appears that modern theology, for all its claim to stress the personal quality of God's revelation to us and our knowledge of Him, actually takes a sub-personal view of both. To maintain that men may know God without God actually speaking to them in words is really to deny that God is personal, or at any rate that knowing Him is a truly personal relationship.

The God of the Bible, however, is a God who talks to men constantly: in visions, dreams, and theophanies; through the

[1] *Westminster Theological Journal*, May 1960 (XXII, ii), pp. 127 f.

prophets, through Christ, through the apostles, and through the written words of Holy Scripture. He talks of His past achievements in creation, judgment, and redemption; He talks of the plans He is currently executing, and of the climax to which He will bring history when the time is ripe; and He talks of human life, telling us what He thinks of the different ways in which men live it, what His own scale of values is, what He likes and what He hates. So, by being propositional, His self-revelation becomes truly personal. And by it God makes friends.

THE PLIGHT OF MAN

Our third question is: what is the state of those to whom God speaks? In what condition does His revelation find them?

The biblical answer is that it finds them ignorant of God. The inscription that Paul saw on the Athenian altar reveals man's natural state: our Maker is to us all 'an unknown God' (Acts 17:23). None of the philosophies that Athens had mothered could help here: 'the world through its wisdom *knew not God*' (I Cor. 1:21; cf. Gal. 4:8; I Thess. 4:5). No man knows God apart from revelation.

The subject of man's ignorance of God is complex. To clarify it, two points must be made in order, as follows.

In the first place, being *creatures*, we cannot know God unless He acts to make Himself known to us. For fifty years before the First World War it was fashionable among theologians to maintain a virtual identity between man's mind and God's, and to try to distil conceptions of the divine nature from our highest thoughts and ideals. It is good that these notions are now generally given up. For the God of the Bible is One whom we can neither see (Jn. 1:18, I Tim. 6:16), nor approach (I Tim. 6:16), nor search out (cf. Job 11: 7, 23: 3–9), and we would fool ourselves if we imagined that we could read His mind, learn His character, guess His motives, or predict His movements, by our own unaided brainwork. 'My thoughts are not your thoughts, neither are your ways my ways, saith the Lord. For as the heavens are higher than the earth, so are my ways higher than your ways, and my thoughts than your thoughts' (Is. 55:8f.). 'How unsearchable are his judgments, and his ways past tracing out!

35

For who hath known the mind of the Lord?' (Rom. 11:33f.). Emil Brunner points the application in a vivid phrase. ' "Canst thou by searching find out God?" To man's proud "not yet" the Bible replies "not ever".'[1] In Scripture it is axiomatic that human thoughts about God which do not depend on revelation are worthless. We can know God only through receiving revelation; not otherwise.

But does not God in fact reveal Himself to all men? How then is it that the world remains ignorant of Him? This brings us to our next point.

In the second place, being *sinful* creatures, we suppress and pervert such revelation from God as reaches us in the ordinary course of life. That God constantly discloses Himself to every one of us as Creator, Lawgiver, and Judge, through nature, providence and the workings of our own mind and conscience, is perfectly true. Awareness of oneself and of the world really does bring an inseparable intuition of the reality of God and His claims. This is usually called 'general' revelation in contrast with 'special' revelation, the historical process recorded in Scripture. The fullest account of general revelation which the Bible gives is in the first two chapters of Romans. There Paul analyses it as God disclosing His eternity, power, and divinity (Rom. 1:20; cf. Ps. 19:1), His kindness (Rom. 2:4, cf. Acts 14:16f.), His moral law (Rom. 2:12ff.), His claim on our worship and homage (1:21), and His condemnation of sin (1:32). As against those who hold that general revelation, and 'natural religion' based on it, can suffice for man without the Bible, we must observe that Paul's analysis shows up the insufficiency of general revelation. It shows us, first, that general revelation is inadequate as a basis for religion, for it yields nothing about God's purpose of friendship with man, nor does it fully disclose His will for human life. Even Adam in Eden needed direct divine speech, over and above general revelation, to make known to him all God's will (cf. Gen. 1:28f. 2:16f.). Second, Paul's analysis shows that general revelation is doubly inadequate to the needs of sinners, for it lacks redemptive content. It indicates that God punishes sin, but not that He pardons it. It shows forgiveness to be needed without showing it to be possible. It preaches the law without the Gospel. It can condemn, but not save. Any unbeliever who rightly understood it

[1] *Our Faith* (London, 1936; 1949 edn.), p. 21.

36

would be driven to despair. However clearly the content of general revelation was grasped, it would by itself provide no adequate basis for fellowship with God.

But in fact we do not find among non-Christians a clear grasp of the content of general revelation. To a greater or less degree, they 'hold down (stifle, *N.E.B.*) the truth in unrighteousness' (Rom. 1:18). This is because they are 'all under sin' (Rom. 3:9). Sin, the ruling force, according to Paul, in every Christless man, is a principle of non-conformity to revelation, and its effects are mental as well as moral. Sin prompts, not only disobedience to God's law, but also denial of His truth. Paul's analysis of general revelation in Romans is part of a great indictment against a sinful world for wilfully darkening the light that general revelation gives. General revelation, he says, is inescapable: 'that which may be known of God is manifest in them (all mankind); for God has manifested it unto them. For the invisible things of him . . . are clearly seen, being perceived through the things that are made . . .' (Rom. 1:19f.). Therefore idolatry and immorality are in every case 'without excuse' (verse 20), for they are always sins against knowledge. The formula explaining their origin is always 'knowing God, they glorified Him not . . . but became vain in their reasonings, and their senseless heart was darkened . . . they became fools and . . . exchanged the truth of God for a lie' ['perverted the truth of God in their lie', H. C. G. Moule] (verses 21-25). Again, in Rom. 2:12-15, Paul appeals to the everyday operations of conscience as showing that all men have received through general revelation some knowledge of God's law. Paul knows that non-Christian consciences act defectively, and are often silent when they ought to speak (cf. Eph. 4:19), but (he says) when they do speak – and every man's conscience, however depraved, speaks sometimes – their method of acting (judging by a standard), the standards to which they appeal, and the actual verdicts they pass, show 'the work of the law written in their hearts' (verse 15). Thus their immoral 'new moralities', and their actual wrongdoings, are without excuse also.

In all this, Paul's point is not that of Aquinas, that the existence of God is abstractly provable by argument from created things, but the much more fundamental point that God's existence and law are actually known to all men, even where both are denied in theory and in practice. Light

37

constantly shines, however much men shut their eyes and pro-
test that they can see nothing. Thus the fact of general revelation proves all men guilty for their irreligion and lawless
living, since all without exception – would they but admit it –
know better.

In fact, some of the light that shines always gets through.
Flashes of true moral and theological insight come to every
non-Christian mind (hence Paul, preaching at Athens, could
appeal to the poet Aratus, Acts 17:28). But these are only
flashes; no more. Calvin compared the isolated insights of the
pagan philosophers to lightning flickering over the benighted.
'Seeing, they saw not. Their discernment was not such as to
direct them to the truth . . . but resembled that of the be-
wildered traveller who sees a lightning-flash glance far and
wide for a moment, and then vanish into the darkness of the
night, before he can advance a single step. So far is such assistance from enabling him to find the right path.'[1] Thus, despite
the occasional truths about God and goodness which general
revelation has planted in his mind, Christless man remains
ignorant of God.

NON-CHRISTIAN RELIGIONS

These considerations throw light on the nature of non-Christian religions. In these days, when Eastern faiths are resurgent,
and Christian missionary advance is slowing down, it is often
asked whether God is not in fact revealed and known outside
Christianity. The question is important, for our whole attitude
to missionary work will depend on our answer to it. Do men of
other faiths know God? A popular view has been that all men
share a basic sense of affinity with God ('the religious *a priori*',
as Continentals call it), that the only ultimate difference between the world's religions lies in the degree of success with
which they cherish and express this innate God-consciousness,
and that what the Bible records is a process of religious evolu-
tion through which man's God-consciousness reached its
supreme expression in the teaching of Jesus (understood, or
rather misunderstood, as essentially a declaration that God is
the Father of all men). On this view, Christianity is certainly
the Rolls-Royce among religions, the best of its kind, but the

[1] Calvin: *Institutes of the Christian Religion*, II, ii, 18.

same basic sense of oneness with God underlies them all, just as the same basic design is found in all cars.

This amounts to saying that all religions, Christianity included, rest entirely on general revelation, which tells us of a basic harmony between God and ourselves – an insight most luminously crystallized in the thought of God as Father. It follows that no one really needs any more knowledge of God than general revelation can give him. But Scripture disagrees. It contrasts Christianity with other faiths at just the point where this theory links them together. Non-biblical religions (it says) are certainly based on general revelation in one sense, but it is general revelation *perverted* and *denied*. Four factors (at least) have conspired to produce them: general revelation, demonic deception (cf. I Cor. 10:20; II Cor. 4:4), the smothering and distorting action of the fallen human mind, and God's judicial giving up of men to the nightmare state of believing what they want to believe and forgetting what they want to forget (Rom. 1:21–23, 25, 28). Non-Christian faiths, therefore, though resulting in one sense from knowledge of God, are actually forms of ignorance of God: modern non-Christians, like the ancient Gentiles, 'know not God' (I Thess. 4:5).

Also, Scripture assures us that apart from the Christian Gospel all thoughts of natural affinity and peace with God are delusive. Where found (and they are not in fact common in non-Christian types of religion) they spring, not from a true reading of general revelation, but from self-deceived wishful thinking. General revelation actually discloses the wrath of God against human sin (Rom 1:18, 32). There is no true knowledge of peace with God outside Christ. In point of fact, the dominant impression which a study of the great non-Christian faiths gives is of an agonized hunger for peace and fellowship with God, a hunger which these religions can evidently deepen but equally evidently cannot satisfy. Not that they are all entirely wrong, or wholly degraded; isolated truths peep through their theology at many points, and the ascetic discipline of the best of them is deeply impressive as an achievement of the human spirit. But in no case is their over-all view of God and of the God-man relationship a true one. In particular, though they have all gained from general revelation some form of belief in cosmic retribution for evil-doing, they none of them know any effective way of reconciliation with the God whom man has offended. They know something of the law, but nothing of the Gospel. They seek peace with God, but, lacking Christ, they cannot find it.

MEN IN DARKNESS

Christless men, then, all the world over, are ignorant of God with an ignorance that is wilful and therefore guilty. 'Since they did not see fit to acknowledge God, God gave them up to a base mind [their own depraved reason, *N.E.B.*] and to improper conduct' (Rom. 1 : 28, R.S.V.) – that is the divine diagnosis of all non-Christian religion and irreligion, and all sub-Christian conduct in the world. Underlying all the observable factors conditioning our beliefs and actions, which the human sciences can and do study, is the act of man refusing to respond to God's light, and the act of God giving him up to intellectual and moral darkness. God in judgment allows recalcitrant man to believe and do what he *likes* – hence all the false faiths and immoralities, pre-Christian, anti-Christian, and post-Christian, which filled the world as Paul knew it, and which still fill it today. (Could there be any account of the state of man, as we know it from our newspapers and our own experience, more shatteringly up-to-date than Rom. 1 : 23–32; Eph. 4 : 17–19; II Tim. 3 : 1–8?)

There is in Anglicanism a strong rationalistic and moralistic tradition of thought, going back beyond last-century liberalism to the seventeenth- and eighteenth-century Latitudinarians 'Latitude-men'), and beyond this to the Platonism of the Renaissance. Its habit is to assume that all men naturally aspire towards God and goodness, to treat the moral and religious intuitions of the educated natural man as ultimate certainties, and to take seriously only those elements of biblical teaching that fit in with them. Naturally, those who stand in this tradition concentrate on ethics, soft-pedal the themes of sin and grace, and tend constantly to endorse in practice the Anabaptist doctrine of salvation by sincerity ('every man shall be saved by the Law or Sect which he professeth, so that he be diligent to frame his life according to that Law, and the light of Nature') – a doctrine which Article XVIII condemns, on the grounds that 'holy Scripture doth set out unto us only the Name of Jesus Christ, whereby men must be saved'. It is this tradition which has led to the taunt that Pelagianism – salvation by

40

moral effort alone – is the Englishman's special heresy! Children of this tradition find it hard to believe that men without Christ are guiltily ignorant of God, perverse more or less in their thoughts of Him, self-idolizers even in their outward worship of Him, and strangers to His friendship. Yet so it is, and it is vitally important that we should face the fact, and admit that, wise and foolish, rich and poor, young and old, white and black, we are by nature all together in this same boat. Even though general revelation shines upon us constantly, we are men in the dark. Apart from special, saving revelation – the revelation that centres upon the Lord Jesus Christ – we do not and cannot know God.

REVELATION TO SINNERS

The nature of revelation as an act of God is now clear. Revelation is our personal Creator and Upholder addressing us in order to make friends with us. We do not find Him; rather, He finds us. He sees us as rebels against Him, with our minds blinded and our characters twisted by sin, actively dishonouring Him by stifling His truth and serving false gods. But His Word addressed to us in Christ, though it begins as bad news, with a disclosure to us of the judgment under which we stand, is essentially good news; for it is a word of pardon and peace, a message of reconciliation by the death of Jesus and of 'a way back to God from the dark paths of sin'.

From this it appears that our study of God's revelation should be controlled by a recognition of two basic truths. The first is that what we are dealing with is a work of grace to sinners, a work, that is, of free undeserved favour towards persons who have forfeited all claim to favour. The Word that God has spoken in His Son concerns a costly and unmerited salvation that God has provided on our behalf. To speak such a word of grace is itself an act of grace, and only those who see revelation as grace can understand it aright.

The second truth to recognize is that knowledge of special revelation can only be drawn from special revelation itself. Only in the light of revelation – God's light, shining into our darkness – can we sin-blinded creatures see light on any spiritual matter. And if we cannot know the truth about God save by revelation, it is surely evident that we cannot know the truth about revelation save by revelation. This means, as

41

we shall see, that the truth about revelation must be learned from the Bible, just as the truth about God's character must be learned from the Bible. We must not be surprised if we find the Bible contradicting our own ideas; nor must we hesitate to recognize that if we depart from the biblical account of revelation, we go wrong. Many Protestant writers today err here, accepting the witness of revelation to other truths yet sitting loose to its witness to itself. Notions such as that revelation took the form of a progress from faulty thoughts of God to more exact ones, or that it took place by divine deed and not by divine word, or that the divine inspiration of statements does not guarantee their truth, or that the scriptural record of revelation is not itself revelation, get copied from book to book without regard for the fact that they contradict revelation's own account of itself. Even 'neo-orthodox' theologians, who rightly stress that revelation is known to us only by its own light, and that the Bible is integral to God's revelatory action, corrupt their understanding of revelation by importing into it rationalistic, non-biblical axioms, such as the allegedly non-propositional character of personal revelation (Brunner) or the alleged paradox that God speaks His infallible word to us through fallacious words of men (Barth). We must be on our guard against such lapses. We only truly honour the God who has spoken in His Son to us blind sinners by listening humbly, teachably, and without interrupting, to what He has to say, and by believing, on His authority, all that He is pleased to tell us – about revelation, no less than any other subject.

CHAPTER THREE

GOD'S WORD SPOKEN (II)

In the last chapter, we thought of God's *general* revelation of Himself as Creator, a revelation given to all men through their own self-awareness and knowledge of God's world (see Rom. 1: 19f.), as well as of His *special* revelation of Himself as Saviour, the revelation which is made known to us in the Gospel (see Rom. 1: 16f.). In this chapter, however, we deal only with the latter.

The second major truth, which the opening words of Hebrews teach us, is that *revelation is a verbal activity*. 'God

. . . hath . . . spoken.' This is not a metaphor for some non-verbal mode of communication; the verb is being used as literally as any human words about God can ever be. The writer means, quite simply, that God has communicated with man by means of significant utterances: statements, questions, and commands, spoken either in His own person or on His behalf by His own appointed messengers and instructors. The rest of the epistle makes this quite plain.

THE PROPHETS

The writer introduces God as 'having of old time spoken unto the fathers in [by, R.S.V., through, N.E.B.] the prophets'. Who and what were the prophets? The most modern New Testament lexicon, that of Arndt-Gingrich, defines the Greek word *prophetes* as 'proclaimer and interpreter of the divine revelation'. The older lexicon of Grimm-Thayer gives a fuller definition: 'one who, moved by the Spirit of God and hence his organ or spokesman, solemnly declares to men what he has received by inspiration, especially future events, and in particular such as relate to the cause and kingdom of God and to human salvation.' These definitions are indisputably correct. In the Hebrew Old Testament, there are three words for prophet: *ro'eh* and *hozeh*, meaning one who sees (a 'seer'), and *nabi* meaning one who calls (a 'crier', like the old English town crier). These words together give us the biblical idea of a prophet. We tend to think of prophets as essentially men who tell the future, but in the Bible the thought of the prophet as predicter is founded on something more basic, namely, the thought of him as a man to whom God speaks and shows things, who is then charged to go and tell others in God's name the things he has seen and heard.

The nature of the prophetic vocation is crystallized in God's words to Jeremiah: 'I have appointed thee a prophet . . . to whomsoever I shall send thee thou shalt go, and whatsoever I shall command thee thou shalt speak . . . *I have put my words in thy mouth*' (Jer. 1:5–9; cf. Is. 6:8ff.; Ezek. 2; Amos 7:14f.). To put words in someone else's mouth is to tell him exactly what to say (see II Sam. 14:3, 19). This was what God did with the prophets. As they repeatedly tell us, 'the word of the Lord came' to them, telling them what they must go and say to others in God's name. Amos describes their position, as mediators of revelation, in two consecutive verses (Amos 3:7f.). 'Surely the Lord God will do nothing, but he revealeth his secret unto his servants the prophets.' There is the prophet as seer and hearer, the recipient of revelation. Then Amos says: 'The lion hath roared, who will not fear? The Lord God hath spoken, who can but prophesy?' There is the prophet as speaker and messenger, constrained to declare the 'secret' that God has shown him. Essentially, therefore, prophets were forthtellers of God's word, human agents through whom He made His statements public and relayed them to the people to whom they were addressed. But because God's 'secret' often included His future plans, as well as the meaning of His present actions, the forthtellers of God's word often appeared as fore-tellers of things to come. That is how the idea of prophets as predicters fits in.

The hallmark of Old Testament prophecy was the prefatory formula: 'Thus saith the Lord.' This formula proclaimed the source and authority of the prophets' messages: it told the world that the things they said were to be heard and received as God's words, His royal announcements, and not just pious productions of man. The prophets' messages corresponded, not to editorials in *The Times*, but to proclamations from Buckingham Palace. Commonly the prophets spoke in God's own person: the 'I' of their oracles is more often than not Jehovah Himself. The psychology of prophetic inspiration, in which auditory, visionary, intuitive, and reflective factors were all involved, is necessarily mysterious to us who do not share it. But both Testaments tell us that, however mysterious, prophetic inspiration was a recurring fact in Israel's history from Moses on, and that this inspiration had definite and characteristic effects. It was more than natural insight, more even than spiritual enlightenment; it was a unique process whereby the human messenger was drawn into such complete identification with the message God had given him to deliver that what he said could be, and indeed had to be, treated as wholly divine. Though the prophet's own powers of thought and craftsmanship were fully exercised in apprehending God's disclosures and, so to speak, preparing them for publication, whether orally or in writing, the resulting product was as uniformly and uncorruptedly 'the word of the Lord' as were the Ten Commandments which Moses received on Sinai, written, we are told, with the finger of God (Ex. 31:18, 32:15f.). The effect of inspiration was that the oracles of the prophets declared, not the prophets' own mind simply, but God's. Nothing that they said 'in the word of the Lord' (I Ki. 13:2, 20:35) might be dismissed in the way that 'all the proud men' dismissed Jeremiah's oracle (Jer. 43:2), as being a mere human mistake. What the prophets said, God said; as Hebrews 1:1 put it, God spoke in and through them, or as II Pet. 1:21 expresses it, 'No prophecy ever came by the will of man; but men spake from God, being moved [impelled, *N.E.B.*] by the Holy Ghost.'

No wonder, then, that the New Testament always treats Old Testament prophecies as true and decisive expressions of God's mind, and finds the chief proof of the divine origin of Christianity in its fulfilment of the prophetic Scriptures (cf. Acts 2:16–36, 3:18ff., 10:43, 13:22ff., 17:2ff., etc.). No wonder that Jesus took Old Testament prophecy as containing His Father's blueprint for His own Messianic ministry, and taught that He had come, not to overthrow the prophets, but to fulfil them (Mt. 5:17; cf. 26:53–56; Lk. 18:3ff., 22:37, 24:25ff., 44ff.; Jn. 13:18, 15:25, 17:12). No wonder that the apostles at once fell into the habit of citing texts from the prophets as utterances of God, or of the Holy Ghost (cf. Acts 1:16, 3:21, 4:24ff., 7:48ff., 13:22, 33–35, 47. 28:25ff.). No wonder that the writer to the Hebrews twice specifies the Holy Spirit as the speaker of particular prophetic messages (3:7 and 10:15, citing Ps. 95:7–11; Jer. 31:33f.).

When our author tells us that in Old Testament times God revealed Himself by speaking the words spoken by the prophets (for that is what it comes to), it is important to see the range of his reference. We are apt today to restrict the term 'prophets' to the authors of the prophetic books of the Old Testament, along with Samuel and his successors in Israel's history. But we need to remember that to the New Testament writers Moses the lawgiver and David and his fellow-psalmists are also among the prophets. The New Testament hails them all as foretellers of Christ (Lk. 24:44; Jn. 5:47; Acts 2:25–31, 7:37). Moses, indeed, was regarded throughout as the supreme prophet (see Deut. 34:10), and the Mosaic body of teaching as the supreme and basic prophetic revelation. When Stephen says that Moses 'received living oracles to give unto us' (Acts 7:38), it is the law of Moses that he has in mind; the law, seen from this standpoint, was entirely prophetic.

45

A further truth to notice here about the things God said through His inspired messengers is that, once spoken, they retained validity and authority for the future. They are to be thought of, therefore, not merely as what God *said*, but as what he *says*. Within the stated range of their application, His promises and threats bind Him, and His commands bind men, as long as the world stands. 'The word of the Lord abideth for ever' (I Pet. 1:25, citing Is. 40:8). 'Till heaven and earth pass away, one jot or one tittle shall in no wise pass away from the law, till all things be accomplished' (Mt. 5:18). Since God's character and plans do not change, it could hardly be otherwise. And as God stands for ever to what He has said, so men in every generation stand under it. The words of the Lord never lose their binding authority. We express our sense of the abiding force of the law of the land by using the present tense when quoting it: 'the law *says*'. In the same way, the writer to the Hebrews expressed his sense of the abiding authority of the words of Ps. 95:7–11 and Jer. 31:33f. by using the present tense when speaking of their divine origin: 'the Holy Ghost (not *said*, but) *saith*' (3:7); 'the Holy Ghost (not *bore*, but) *beareth* witness to us' (10:15).

Not, of course, that the New Testament writers regard all the Old Testament words of God as retaining their original application. They interpret them, not in terms of the old, preparatory, typical dispensation under which they were spoken, and to which in most cases they had immediate reference, but christologically – that is, they reapply them in terms of the new situation created by the fulfilling of prophecy in the life, death, resurrection, and reign of the Lord Jesus Christ. The way in which, as we saw, Hebrews interprets Ps. 95:7ff. and Jer. 31:33f. as testimony by the Holy Ghost to New Testament Christians is a case in point. Accordingly, the New Testament recognizes that some requirements of the Mosaic law were only meant for the old covenant epoch, and were never intended by God to bind Christians: the law of circumcision, for instance (cf. Acts 15 and Galatians), or the Levitical festal calendar (cf. Gal. 4:10; Col. 2:16–23), or the sacrificial cultus (cf. Heb. 7–10, 13:9–16). The coming of Christ superseded these typical ordinances, and the divine instruction which Christians are to draw from them concerns, not God's will for their own present action, but the truths concerning God, man, and Christ, which the observing of these ordinances was always intended to inculcate upon Israelite minds. It is in this sense – that is, as witnesses to doctrine – that these sections of the Old Testament law abide in force. We must remember that in the biblical conception of law (Hebrew, *torah*, literally 'instruction') theological teaching and ethical enactment are organically united, so that legislative amendments which confirm the original theological teaching could not be held in any significant sense to 'destroy' the law (cf. Mt. 5:17).

THE OLD TESTAMENT

We have not yet done with the witness of the author of Hebrews to the verbal character of revelation. We must now observe that he regards, not only individual prophetic and legislative oracles, but the whole Old Testament, as verbal revelation from God. This appears from a fact which makes his letter unique in the New Testament – namely, that he bases his whole argument, from start to finish, on Old Testament passages; all of which he treats as prophetic in the sense explained, that is, as authoritative disclosures of God's mind, even though some of them (those in 1:6–12, 2:6ff., and 12:5f.) are not, in their original contexts, words spoken by God in His own person. Thus, in chapter 1, the deity and kingship of God's Son are set forth on the basis of an appeal in verses 5–13 to Ps. 2:7, II Sam. 7:14, Deut. 32:43 (a part of the text which was only known from the Septuagint version till the Hebrew original was recently found at Qumran), Pss. 45:6f., 102:25ff., 110:1. Chapter 2 speaks of the manhood of the King in the light of Ps. 8:4ff. (itself an echo of Gen. 1:28), which is cited in verses 6ff. In chapters 3 and 4, an expository application of Ps. 95:7–11 is made, to show the need for believing adherence to the Gospel. In chapters 5 and 7, the Melchizedek priesthood of Jesus is expounded from Ps. 110:4. Chapter 6 treats briefly (verses 12–19) of God's faithfulness to His promises, the point being made by appeal in verse 14 to God's promises to Abraham, recorded in Gen. 22:16. In chapters 8 and 10, the fulfilment of Jeremiah's new covenant prophecy (Jer. 31:31–34) is announced and explained. In chapter 9, the meaning of Christ's sacrifice is shown from the significance of God's directions, enjoined upon Moses in Ex. 25:40 (cited, Heb. 8:5), for the structure and service of the tabernacle. Chapter 10 invokes Deut. 32:35ff. and Hab. 2:3f. (verses 30, 27) to underline the danger of apostasy and the need for steadfastness. Chapter 11 ranges widely through Old Testament narratives of how God spoke to His servants, and how they responded, in order to make the point that faith is a practical embracing of God's promises and adhering to them against all odds. Chapter 12 deals with the place of chastisement in the Christian life, by generalizing from Prov. 3:11f., cited in verses 5f. Chapter 13 sets forth the basis of Christian contentment in God's promise to Joshua (Josh. 1:5), which is quoted in verse 5 and followed by Ps. 118:6, as expressing our proper response to it.

Clearly, to this writer (and the whole New Testament is with him) the sentences and sentiments of the Old Testament are so many units of divine instruction, true testimonies to God's will, works, and ways, proceeding, in the last analysis, from His own mouth. The epistle to the Hebrews thus impressively illustrates what it means to believe that 'all scripture is inspired by God and (therefore) profitable for teaching, for reproof, for correction, for instruction in righteousness' (II Tim. 3:16, R.S.V.). The writer's position is that not only the words of the prophets, but the entire Old Testament, first to last, is 'God's Word written' – that is, verbal revelation.

REVELATION IN CHRIST

Then the writer tells us that God has now spoken 'in His Son'. Some today argue as if revelation in the person of Christ takes us beyond the realm of verbal revelation altogether. But our author does not think so; rather, he regards verbal revelation as of the essence of our Lord's own revelatory ministry. This appears from his reference in 2:3 to the 'great salvation' which 'having at the first been *spoken* through the Lord, was confirmed unto us by them that *heard* him'. Here he focuses our attention on the verbal instruction – the 'word' – which Jesus and His apostles gave men in the Father's name. In this, be it noted, our author was simply following in Jesus' own footsteps: for Jesus Himself regularly reduced the question of whether men perceived God's saving revelation in Him to the question of whether they received and responded to His instruction, as to divine truth. (On the divine origin of Jesus' 'word', see Jn. 3:14, 34, 7:16f., 8:26, 28, 38, 40, 43 with 47, 12:49f.,

14: 10, 24, 15: 15, 17: 8, 14, 18: 37. On the implications of receiving or rejecting it, see Mt. 7: 21–27; Lk. 6: 46–49, 8: 4–21, 11: 28; Jn. 3: 11, 8: 31, 37, 43, 47, 12: 48, 14: 21–23, 15: 7, 17: 6–8, 18: 37.) Also, the writer is chiming in with the claims of Paul; for Paul announced his Gospel as God's long-hidden 'mystery' [secret], now made known to Christ's 'apostles and prophets' by revelation (Eph. 3: 3–5; Rom. 16: 25ff., cf. Gal. 1: 12; I Cor. 2: 10–13), so that it was 'not . . . the word of man, but . . . in truth, the word of God' (I Thess. 2: 13). For himself, Paul's claim was that by virtue of his apostolic enduement with the Holy Spirit (cf. I Cor. 2: 12f.) he spoke as Christ's mouth, just as the prophets had spoken as God's mouth. Thus his evangelical teaching really was God's pure truth (cf. Gal. 1: 6ff.) and his injunctions really were 'commandments of the Lord' (I Cor. 14.37). (On the divine source and truth of the apostles' 'word', see also Jn. 14: 26, 15: 26f., 16: 12–15, 17: 20; and cf. Rev. 1: 1–3, 19, 22: 6–9, 18f.). This array of evidence compels us to recognize that revelation in Christ, however great an advance it marked on what had gone before, did not involve any breach of the principle that what God reveals is made known to men by means of verbal instruction from God Himself.

Accordingly, at the end of the letter to the Hebrews, having referred to the 'voice of words' which Israel heard at Sinai (12: 19), the writer sums up his appeal thus: 'See that ye refuse not him that *speaketh*. For if they escaped not, when they refused him that *warned* them upon earth, much more shall not we escape, who turn away from him that *warneth* from heaven: whose voice then shook the earth: but now he hath *promised, saying*, yet once more will I make to tremble not the earth only, but also the heaven' (12: 25f., citing Hag. 2: 6). The italicized words make it clear beyond all shadow of doubt that to this writer (and, once more, he has the whole New Testament with him) the essence of the Christian revelation is verbal communication from God, conveyed through Christ and His apostles.

VERBAL REVELATION UNDER CRITICISM

We have now reached the first of the watersheds at which the streams divide in modern discussions of revelation. The cleavage comes over whether or not we think of revelation as the writer to the Hebrews does, as divine verbal communication, God using human language, spoken and written by His special messengers, to make His mind, and so Himself, known to mankind. Many today hold views of revelation in history and in experience which move them, not merely to reject this idea, but to attack it, as positively harmful. This being so, it is important to be clear on just what the apostolic position does and does not involve.

First, some negatives, made necessary by current misconceptions.

1. The idea of revelation as essentially verbal communication does not imply the concept of God as a celestial rabbi who does nothing but sit and talk. It does not, therefore, cut across the stress which modern theology rightly lays on the fact that the God of the Bible (and, of course, of Hebrews!) is a living, active Being, the Lord and Maker of history, who discloses Himself by means of mighty acts of redemption; and that the Bible itself is essentially a recital of His doings, an explanatory narrative of the great drama of the bringing in of His kingdom, and the saving of the world.[1] Belief that the mode of revelation is verbal is in no way inconsistent with recognizing that the subject-matter of revelation is the living God and His redeeming work, as the epistle to the Hebrews itself shows plainly enough.

2. Nor does this belief imply that the receiving of revelation is simply a matter of sitting down and learning biblical doctrines. It is ironical when holders of the Hebrews position are accused of intellectualizing and depersonalizing faith. No modern theologian could make the point that faith is not orthodoxy alone, but 'existential' trust in the living God, more forcibly than Hebrews 11 does. In fact, as we observed earlier, and as Hebrews 11 shows (verses 7, 8, 11, 13, etc.), such trust is only possible on the basis of verbal communications

[1] This emphasis, characteristic of the British 'biblical theology' movement and the continental 'Heilsgeschichte' theologians (cf., on the latter, Alan Richardson: *The Bible in the Age of Science* [London, 1961], pp. 122 ff.), finds typical expression in such books as Gabriel Hebert: *The Bible from Within* (Oxford, 1950); William Neil: *The Rediscovery of the Bible* (London, 1954); Oscar Cullman: *Christ and Time* (Eng. tr., London, 1951); G. E. Wright: *God Who Acts* (London, 1952); and in the Committee Report on the Holy Bible at the 1958 Lambeth Conference (*The Lambeth Conference 1958*, 2, 2 ff., especially pp. 9–12).

from God – divine commands and promises – recognized as such.

3. Nor does the belief that revelation is essentially verbal communication from heaven militate in any way against the New Testament identification of Jesus as Himself the Word of God (Jn. 1:1–14) who discloses the Father (Jn. 1:18, 14:9). To argue otherwise, as some do, is like arguing that, because 'Flying Scotsman' is the name of a locomotive, it cannot also be the name of a train. 'Word' (*logos*) denotes the expression of mind in reasoning and speech. God's Son is called His 'Word' because in Him God's mind, character, and purposes find full expression. God's revelation is called His 'Word' because it is reasoned verbal discourse which has God as its subject and its source. The verbal 'Word' bears witness to the personal 'Word', and enables us to know the latter for what He is, which otherwise we could not do. There is no inconsistency here. It is noticeable that, though Hebrews begins by hailing God's Son as the perfect image of His Father (1:3), three times out of four the phrase 'Word of God' is used to denote, not Christ, but the divine message concerning Him (4:12, 6:5, 13:7). (For other uses of 'Word' in Hebrews for God's verbal communications to men, see 2:2, 4:2, 7:28, 12:19.)

But what the claim that revelation is essentially verbal does imply is that no historical event, as such, can make God known to anyone unless God Himself discloses its meaning and place in His plan. Providential happenings may serve to remind us, more or less vividly, that God is at work (cf. Acts 14:17), but their link, if any, with His saving purpose cannot be known until He Himself informs us of it. No event is self-interpreting at this level. The Exodus, for instance, was only one of many tribal migrations that history knows (cf. Amos 9:7); Calvary was only one of many Roman executions. Whoever could have guessed the unique saving significance of these events, had not God Himself spoken to tell us? All history is, in one sense, God's deed, but none of it reveals Him except in so far as He Himself talks to us about it. God's revelation is not through deeds without words (a dumb charade!) any more than it is through words without deeds; but it is through deeds which He speaks to interpret, or, putting it more biblically, through words which His deeds confirm and fulfil. The fact we must face is that if there is no verbal revelation, there is no revelation at all, not even in the life, death, and resurrection of Jesus of Nazareth.

A CURRENT ALTERNATIVE

This point is crucial for current debate, since the view of revelation which, following writers like William Temple and Leonard Hodgson,[1] most British theologians now seem to hold in one form or another, really depends on denying it. According to this view, God revealed Himself in history by illuminating chosen observers of significant events so that they perceived what the events meant, in terms of God's character and plan. The events thus gained revelatory status through the coincidence with them of divinely enlightened minds. But this enlightening, though it heightened the observers' intuitive and reflective capacities, and sharpened their moral and spiritual perceptions, was not in itself an infusing into their minds of truths from God. As Temple put it: 'There is no such thing as revealed truth. There are truths of revelation, that is to say propositions which express the results of correct thinking concerning revelation; but they are not themselves directly revealed.'[2]

Many find this view appealing because, while it purports to safeguard the reality of revelation in history, it does not oblige us to treat all the contents of Scripture as truths of revelation. Fallible men, however enlightened, may yet make factual and theological mistakes, and on this view we have no reason to regard biblical authors as exceptions to the rule. Thus this teaching comes to terms with the methods of conventional Protestant biblical criticism, which for over a century has worked on the basis of a deliberate rejection of the idea of inerrancy. Those who take Temple's approach are thereby set free to enthrone historical criticism as the basic technique of Christian theology; and it appears that the number of those who see the theologian's task as, first, to reconstruct biblical history ('what *really* happened') from the biblical narratives, and then, in the light of this reconstruction, to assess the adequacy of the interpretations of this history which the biblical writers propound,

[1] See Temple: *Nature, Man and God* (London, 1934), Lecture xii, and his essay in *Revelation*, ed. D. M. Baillie and H. Martin (London, 1937); Hodgson: *The Doctrine of the Trinity* (London, 1943), Lecture i.

[2] *Nature, Man, and God*, p. 317.

is now large.[1] But the approach itself is vulnerable on many grounds.

First, it effectively overthrows the whole biblical idea of knowing God, having fellowship with God, and being God's friend. It holds that God's way of making Himself known, both to the biblical writers and to ourselves, is not to address words to any of us, but simply to guide our minds into right thoughts about Him as we watch Him in action. But this cannot in principle yield *personal* knowledge of God at all. As a Gloucestershire boy, I knew all about Walter Hammond, and when I saw him in action I had enough insight into cricket to tell why he swung his bat the way he did. But I was never a friend of his, for I never knew him personally; he never spoke to me. On the basis of the view under discussion, we should have to conclude that no one, in Bible times or since, has ever had personal acquaintance with God, and, further, that the biblical idea of communion and friendship with God within a covenant relationship, in which He is committed to me as my God by promise, is an unrealizable dream.

Second, this view overthrows the biblical idea of faith, which is essentially of honouring God by tenaciously trusting to what He has *said*. When Abraham, whom the New Testament hails as the man of faith *par excellence*, 'believed God, and it was reckoned unto him for righteousness' (Rom. 4:3; Gal. 3:6, citing Gen. 15:6), the object of his faith was a specific promise. (See also Heb. 6:13ff., 11:8–13, 17.) Hebrews 11:33 says that the Old Testament heroes 'through faith . . . obtained promises'; but if the teaching under discussion is the whole truth about revelation, there never were any promises for them to obtain, or us either.

Third, this view compels the conclusion that God never in fact addressed words to any prophet or apostle at any stage, so that all their recorded experiences of hearing his voice must

[1] Thus, for instance, George Every writes of Herbert Kelly: 'In his own reflections on the Old Testament Father Kelly had a way of going directly to the event, without even noticing the interpretation given by the prophet or the prophetic historian' (H. Kelly: *The Gospel of God* [London, 1959 ed.], p. 34). In this Kelly was showing himself less a prophet to our time than a child of it. D. B. Knox comments: 'It will be seen that if revelation is in the event rather than in the interpretation, revelation becomes like a nose of wax to be re-shaped according to every man's whim' ('Propositional Revelation the Only Revelation': *Reformed Theological Review*, February 1960 [XIX, 1], p. 5).

be dismissed, as C. H. Dodd dismisses the divine words of commissioning which Jeremiah heard, as 'actual hallucinations'.[1] This implies that, whatever they, in their hallucinatory state, may have believed about the source of their messages, we should never take their 'thus saith the Lord . . .' as really meaning more than: 'I feel quite certain that if God spoke He would say . . .' Accordingly we must understand their authority, not as that of God speaking through them directly, but rather of themselves as theological pundits and religious experts, sharing with us their own beliefs about One who, though active in other ways, is dumb, and never speaks for Himself. But all this is highly unbiblical.

Then, fourth, this view overlooks the fact that in the case of all events of importance in the history of salvation (not to speak of many others), God did not leave their significance to be perceived during or after their occurrence, but prefaced them, often at a very long range, by verbal predictions of what he was in due course going to do. This happened, we are told, in the case of the Exodus, the conquest of Canaan, the setting up of the kingdom, the exile, the return, the coming of Christ, the Cross and resurrection, the sending of the Spirit, the calling of the Gentiles – the list could be lengthened further. These are facts with which the theory under review cannot cope; it can only be saved, therefore, by wholesale denial that these predictions ever really took place. Thus the theory disallows the claim made in Isaiah 46:9f., 'I am God, and there is none like me; declaring the end from the beginning, and from ancient times things that are not yet done . . .' If Temple's theory stands, then not only is this claim not a revealed truth, it is not even a truth of revelation.

Fifth, if there are no revealed truths, then the theological statements made by the Lord Jesus Christ are not revealed truths; and what, in that case, are we to make of His solemn assertions, 'my teaching is not mine, but his that sent me'; 'as the Father hath taught me, I speak these things'; 'the Father which sent me, he hath given me a commandment, what I should say, and what I should speak . . . even as the Father hath said unto me, so I speak'; 'as I hear, I judge'; 'I speak the things which I have seen with my Father . . . the truth, which I heard from God'; 'my words shall not pass away' (Jn. 7:16, 8:28, 12:49f., 5:30, 8:38ff.; Mk. 13:31)? Did

[1] *The Authority of the Bible* (London, 1960 ed.), p. 83.

our Lord suffer from hallucinations? Did the Father, after all, never speak to His Son? A theory that fails to allow for even the possibility that the words of Jesus have the status of verbal revelation surely stands self-condemned.

Further objections might be brought, but it already seems plain that this theory is untenable, and so we forbear.

GOD REVEALED THROUGH HIS WORDS

It will be helpful to set alongside this unbiblical, indeed anti-biblical, theory a recapitulation of the position that we ourselves are arguing.[1] This may be summed up as follows:

What is revelation? From one standpoint it is God's act, from another His gift. From both standpoints it is correlative to man's knowledge of God, as on the one hand an experience and on the other a possession. As God's act, revelation is the personal self-disclosure whereby He brings us actively and experimentally to know Him as our own God and Saviour. As God's gift, revelation is the knowledge about Himself which He gives us as a means to this end. Revelation as God's act takes place through the bestowing of revelation as God's gift; the first sense of the word thus comprehends the second. Accordingly, revelation in the narrower sense ought always to be studied in the setting of revelation in the broader sense.

How does God reveal what has to be revealed in order that we may know Him? By verbal communication from Himself. Without this, revelation in the full and saving sense cannot take place at all. For no public historical happening, as such (an exodus, a conquest, a captivity, a crucifixion, an empty tomb), can reveal God apart from an accompanying word from God to explain it, or a prior promise which it is seen to confirm or fulfil. Revelation in its basic form is thus of necessity propositional; God reveals Himself by telling us about Himself, and what He is doing in His world. The statement in Hebrews 1:1, that in Old Testament days God spoke 'in divers manners', reminds us of the remarkable variety of means whereby, according to the record, God's communications were

[1] See further my *Fundamentalism and the Word of God* (London, 1958); 'Revelation and Inspiration' in *The New Bible Commentary* (2nd ed., London, 1954), pp. 21ff.; article 'Revelation', in the *The New Bible Dictionary* (London, 1962).

55

on occasion given: theophanies, angelic announcements, an audible voice from heaven (Ex. 19:9; Mt. 3:17, II Pet. 1:17), visions, dreams, signs, the sacred lot (Urim and Thummim: I Sam. 28:6), supernatural writing (Ex. 31:18, Dan. 5:5), inward locutions, and what from the outside looks rather like clairvoyance (cf. I Sam. 9:15–10:9), as well as the more organic type of inspiration, whereby the Spirit of God so controlled the reflective operations of men's minds as to lead them to a right judgment in all things. But in every case the disclosures introduced, or conveyed, or confirmed, by these means were propositional in substance and verbal in form.

Why does God reveal Himself to us? Because, as we saw, He who made us rational beings wants, in His love, to have us as His friends; and He addresses His words to us – statements, commands, promises – as a means of sharing His thoughts with us, and so of making that personal self-disclosure which friendship presupposes, and without which it cannot exist.

What is the content of God's revelation? This is determined primarily by our present plight as sinners. Though we have lapsed into ignorance of God and a godless way of life, God has not abandoned His purpose to have us as His friends; instead, He has resolved in His love to rescue us from sin and restore us to Himself. His plan for doing this was to make Himself known to us as our Redeemer and Re-creator, through the incarnation, death, resurrection, and reign of His Son. The working out of this plan required a long series of preparatory events, starting with the promise to the woman's seed (Gen. 3:15) and spanning the whole of Old Testament history. Also, it required a mass of concurrent verbal instruction, predicting each item in the series before it came and applying its lessons in retrospect, so that at each stage men might understand the unfolding history of salvation, hope in the promise of its full accomplishment, and learn what manner of persons they, as objects of grace, ought to be. Thus the history of salvation (the acts of God) took place in the context of the history of revelation (the oracles of God).

But the epoch of revelation ended with Christ and the apostles: how, then, does God reveal Himself to us today? By saying to us the same things that He said to others long ago, only now in direct application to ourselves, in the situation in which we are. The biblical idea, as we saw, is that God's words, spoken at particular moments in biblical history, have binding force for all succeeding generations. He does not change; and therefore His assertions, once made, remain true, to govern every man's thinking. The judgments He once passed on particular individuals or groups stand for ever as a revelation of His character and of the standards by which He measures us all. Similarly, His moral instruction remains valid as declaring His ideals for all our lives. God's historical utterances thus operate like statute law in society. Enactments of various dates, once on the statute book, remain continually in force, applying in principle to everyone (though it may need hard thinking and careful arguing to show just how), and each generation is obliged to comply with what 'the law says'. In the same way, we are all under obligation to God, to do as His words, spoken at different times in biblical history, require – or, as we put it, to be ruled by what 'the word of God says'.

The utterances of God thus function (to change the illustration) like the words of a university tutor in a group tutorial, where one person brings and reads an essay and the rest of the group learns by hearing the tutor's comments on it. As the history of the words of God passes before us in our Bible reading and our hearing of sermons, it is as if we were in a group tutorial with Abraham, Moses, David, Elijah, Peter, the Israelites, the Christians of Rome, the Galatian believers, the seven churches of the Apocalypse, and all the rest of those to whom particular words of God were addressed, and with whom His dealings are recorded. We overhear what God is saying to them as He comments on what they have done and gives them advice and guidance for the future, and from this we learn what He would say to us about our own lives. And, just as the listener in a joint tutorial under a shrewd teacher who knows his pupils will often feel, and with reason, that the comments called forth by the essay have been 'angled' to give needed instruction to all present as well as to the essayist himself, so the Christian studying the recorded words of God will often feel that what God said to someone thousands of years ago speaks to his own condition so perfectly that it might have been written specially for him. (And so, of course, it was! – for, just as every Christian can truly say, with Paul, that Christ 'loved me, and gave Himself for me' (Gal. 2:20), so he can truly say that God 'loved me, and wrote this book for me'. What God caused to be written for the Church in general (cf. I Cor. 10:11; Rom. 15:4) He caused to be written for each Christian individually. The devotional maxim that one should read the Scriptures as one would read a personal letter from one's best friend, rests not on pious fancy, but on the hardest theological fact.)

The final truth which the opening words of Hebrews teach is that *revelation is a cumulative activity*. God's revelation in Christ does not stand alone, but comes as the climax of a long series of revelatory disclosures. The statement that in Old Testament times God spoke (as the *New English Bible* put it) 'in fragmentary and varied fashion through the prophets' covers the earlier items in the series. 'But in this the final age', the same version continues, 'he has spoken to us in the Son.'

'In fragmentary and varied fashion . . . in the Son . . .' Here is implied, not only a climax, but also a contrast between a revelation, or series of revelations, that was partial and incomplete, a thing of bits and pieces, not fully integrated, and a revelation that was comprehensive, unified, and final. How should we interpret this contrast? The rest of the epistle shows us. It is the contrast, not between crude and refined, 'primitive' and 'evolved', partly false and wholly true, but between promises and their fulfilment, types and their antitype, shadows and substance, incompleteness and perfection, in the two successive dispensations of divine grace under which God's covenant people have successively lived. It is a contrast to be expounded in terms, not of better conceptions of God, but of the better covenant (Heb. 7 : 22), the better priest (7 : 26ff.), the better sacrifice (9.23), the better promises (8 : 6), the better hope (7 : 19), the fuller access (9 : 8f., 10 : 19ff.), and the livelier foretastes of glory (6 : 4f.), that Christians have through Christ as compared with Old Testament believers; as also in terms of the fact that the Gospel of Christ is for Jew and Gentile alike, whereas the Old Testament revelation was addressed to Jews only (cf. Ps. 147 : 19f.). The phrase 'in fragmentary . . . fashion' ('by divers portions') denotes simply, as John Owen saw long ago, that 'the will of God concerning His worship and obedience, was not formerly revealed all at once to His Church, by Moses or any other', but that its revelation was a gradual process, 'by the addition of one thing after another, at several seasons, as the Church could bear the light of them, and as it was subserving to His main design of reserving all pre-eminence to the Messiah'.[1] Then, in New Testament times, just as all roads were said to lead to Rome, so all the diverse and seemingly divergent strands of Old Testament revelation were found to lead to Jesus Christ, prophet, priest, and king, mediator, sacrifice, and intercessor, crucified, risen, and coming again.

Since the New Testament represents in these ways an advance on the Old, may we not speak of revelation as progressive? It all depends on what we mean by 'progressive'. If our meaning is simply that God's Old Testament utterances, however diverse, all contributed in one way or another to His 'build-up' for the coming of His Son, the word is acceptable enough. But much liberal theology has used the word to express the idea that the history of revelation is really the history of how Israel's thoughts of God evolved from something very crude (a tribal war-god) through something more refined (a moral Creator) to the conception of God taught by Jesus (a loving Father); and has set forth this idea in such a way as to imply that Christians need not bother with the Old Testament at all, since all that is true in its view of God can be learned from the New Testament, and all the rest of what it says about Him is more or less false. But this is not so. God was certainly amplifying men's knowledge about Himself throughout the revelatory process, but the idea that what was revealed later contradicts and cancels what was revealed earlier is wrong. So is the widespread neglect of the Old Testament to which this idea has led. The New Testament revelation rests at every point on the Old as its foundation, and to remove the foundation once the superstructure is in place is the surest way to dislodge the superstructure itself. Those who neglect the Old Testament will never make much of the New. When, therefore, the phrase 'progressive revelation' is used as a label for this myth of evolutionary religious development, and hence as a justification for disregarding the Old Testament, it is false, and since the word 'progressive' has been pressed into service so often in this sense, it is best to eschew it – simply to avoid confusion – when stating the biblical position. The belief that later revelation, so far from conflicting with what had gone before, presupposed it and built on it at each stage, is best

[1] Commentary on *Hebrews*, ad loc. (London, 1840 ed., Vol. II, pp. 20, 19).

expressed by calling the revelatory process 'cumulative', rather than 'progressive'.

But if the process of revelation in history over a thousand years and more was cumulative, and if the later items in the series of God's words built on those that had gone before, then it is clear that these later items can only be interpreted in the light of the series as a whole, and in particular that the last item of all – God's Word spoken by His Son – is further from being self-interpreting than any, and needs to be set in the context of all God's earlier words before it can be properly understood. Which means that the very nature of the revelatory process itself made it necessary that a unified record of God's words should be provided. Just as, if we sinners were ever to know God as our Friend, He had to speak to us about redemption, so, if the sequence of His words was to have its intended effect upon us, there had to be a total presentation of it in permanently accessible form – in other words, there had to be a Bible. Confirmation of this reasoning lies in the fact that God actually has given us just such a Bible – a book made up of many books, which grew to its present size in step with the ongoing revelatory process itself, and which now stands as a full explanatory narrative of the saving words and deeds of God. As Calvin put it, 'in order that, with the constant forward march of divine instruction (*continuo progressu doctrinae*), God's truth might remain a survivor in the world in all ages, He willed that the oracles which He had deposited with the fathers should be, so to speak, consigned to public records.'[1] So the Bible, a book thrown up by the revelatory process in history, was no accidental by-product of that process, but an integral and indispensable part of it; for without a record of God's earlier revelations, His later words and, most of all, His last Word, could not be fully understood. Nor, without a permanent record of the whole process, could God's revelation as a whole be preserved against corruption to do in each generation its own proper work of bringing sinners to know God.

[1] *Institutes*, I, vi. 2.

CHAPTER FOUR

GOD'S WORD WRITTEN

IN this chapter, we shall sketch in the view of Holy Scripture to which the last two chapters have been pointing – which is, in fact, in all essentials the view embodied in our historic Reformed standards.[1] To clear our path, we start with some further comments on the 'critical' study of Scripture, as practised today.

THE 'CRITICAL' METHOD

What marks off the 'critical' movement, so-called, from the biblical scholarship of earlier days is that it approaches the Bible first and foremost as a book of ancient history, and studies it in the light of a view of history as a developing process with its own causal laws inherent in itself – a view which came of age as one of the secularized, 'scientific' speculations which filled the German universities in the last century. Accordingly, biblical study in Protestant centres of learning, as witness their textbooks and examination papers, is now dominated by, on the one hand, minute inquiry into the sources, dates, authorship, occasion, and purpose, of the various biblical books, and, on the other hand, attempts to reconstruct from the 'modern' point of view, as an intelligible self-contained process, the sequence of events which the Bible itself narrates as the story of God's work in creation, providence, and grace.

It is clear that this method, as described, squares more easily with a naturalistic, evolutionary, anti-miraculous, uniformitarian outlook than it does with any form of the belief that biblical and church history, while conditioned at all points by prior factors which historians can tabulate, has actually been *caused* by repeated intrusions (revelatory, miraculous, regenerative) of the power of God in *new creation*, intrusions which produce in the lives of men and nations effects that are ultimately inexplicable in terms of what went before. And in fact the pioneers of historical biblical criticism linked their

[1] See pp. 21ff. above.

enterprise so closely to anti-supernatural axioms, including a dogmatic denial of biblical inerrancy, that an impression was created that biblical study would not be 'scientific' at all, in any sense, if done on any other basis. From this secular superstition – for such it is – later Protestant scholarship has never quite broken free. (Its Roman counterpart, which, though embracing the historical approach, cleaves to an explicit supernaturalism and an equally explicit doctrine of biblical inerrancy, does better at this point.[1]) Today, most English Protestant scholars, more conservative, as ever, than their opposite numbers in Germany and America, guardedly accept the miraculous, and maintain, however blurrily, the broad outlines of the biblical faith; but almost to a man they still execrate the doctrine of inerrancy. Meanwhile, 'biblical criticism' remains identified in many Christian minds with an unlawful craving to tone down the Bible and justify unorthodox beliefs, and so continues suspect.

It needs to be said clearly that, though such distorting pseudo-scientific assumptions as those mentioned must certainly be rejected, the use of an historical method of studying Scripture is a theological necessity none the less. For God's revelation really did take the form of an historical process; God's Word concerning it really does take the form of a book of ancient history; the reality of biblical inspiration does imply that we learn God's message through finding out what the human writers meant (for what they said, He says); and unless we understand their statements historically – in terms, that is, of their intended meaning when first made – we are bound to misunderstand them, more or less. This was the point of the Reformers' insistence that Scripture must be interpreted 'literally', as opposed to allegorically. Their plea was for what in the American tongue is known as 'grammatico-historical' exegesis – a technique of which, by common consent, John Calvin himself was as great a master as the Church ever had. The truth is that, as Jesus of Nazareth was no less truly human than divine, so it is with the Scriptures. The mystery of the Word incarnate is at this point parallel to that of the Word

---

[1] Modern Roman achievement in this field may be gauged by two books which, apart from their inevitable weaknesses regarding justification and the Church, are in the main very fine: C. Charlier: *The Christian Approach to the Bible* (Eng. tr., London, 1958); L. Bouyer: *The Meaning of Sacred Scripture* (Eng. tr., Indiana and London, 1960).

written. And as we must see Jesus in His human, historical context, and study His recorded words as the sayings of a first-century Jew, if we would fully grasp their message to us as words of God, so it is in interpreting all the words of the Bible. Therefore inquiry into the linguistic, cultural, historical, and theological background of the various parts of Holy Scripture, and into the outlook and aims of their respective authors, must be welcomed as a necessary discipline if the Bible is to be rightly understood. Historical criticism, then, though in the past abused, is really essential; there can be no good commentaries, or accurate exposition, or sound theology, without it. We do well to remember at this point that the proper meaning of 'criticism' is not *censure*, as such, but *appreciation*. It would be as misguided to discourage appreciative study of the human aspects of Scripture, for fear of losing our grip on its divinity, as it would be to discourage frank recognition of the manhood of our Lord on similar grounds. The only proviso is that our study of the Bible, as of Christ Himself, must be based on fully biblical presuppositions about that which we are studying.

SOME INADEQUATE POSITIONS

Those who, following the current conventions of criticism, reject Augustine's axiom that what Scripture says, God says, divide sharply over the questions of how God's truth reaches us, and what its content is. Thus, for instance, Anglican 'broad churchmen' in the Platonist tradition, like the authors of *Essays and Reviews* in the last century and, as it seems, for all his borrowed biblicist and existentialist plumage, the author of *Honest to God* in this, think of revelation in terms of a quickening of conscience to embrace moral and spiritual imperatives on the basis of a robust cosmic optimism – a belief, that is, that goodness will triumph in the end, or love will be the last word, or something similar. Revelation, on this view, certainly occurs through contact with the Bible, but the communicated content is only a slice off the Bible; in particular, the event of revelation does not necessarily lead to a positive avowing of apostolic theology, as such, as divine truth, or to any clear link between the doctrine of grace and Christian ethical imperatives comparable to that which we find in the epistles of Paul. This outlook is not unlike that of the old Continental Liberalism, which was based, not on Platonism, but on positivism; both views in practice by-pass the apostles and concentrate on the Jesus of the gospels as teacher, pioneer, and example of the good life.

By contrast, 'dialectical' theologians like Barth, Brunner, and Niebuhr, hold that the Word of God in Christ with which the Bible confronts us is a reality which has to be set forth in the categories of apostolic teaching about sin and salvation – though this, they say, does not oblige us to echo the apostles at every point, since details of the apostolic witness to the Word of God sometimes need correcting and improving. Those in this camp would all say that Jesus Christ rather than Scripture is the Word of God (an improper antithesis, as we saw); but if we ask them, on this basis, to give us an account of Jesus Christ, and to tell us how the two Testaments belong together, and how the Christ of apostolic faith stands related to the Jesus of historical fact, their unanimity dissolves at once into a shambles of conflicts and confusions.

A third, 'existentialist', type of view, popular at present through the work of Bultmann and Tillich, is that the Word of God is, strictly speaking, neither Holy Scripture nor Jesus Christ, but God confronting the individual in a way which produces within him a liberating assurance, assuaging his otherwise incurable *angst* (restless anxiety). This assurance – 'openness to the future', Bultmann calls it – is equated with faith. It does not come without our contemplating the (largely unhistorical and mythological) New Testament witness to Jesus, but it is none the less consistent with denying Jesus' personal deity, pre-existence, virgin birth, miracles, bodily resurrection, and indeed every bit of information about Him that the New Testament gives us save the bare fact that He was crucified.

It is clear that such 'faith' is not very different from the unfocused cosmic optimism of the Anglican 'broad church' outlook – which perhaps helps to explain how the author of *Honest to God* could feel at home with Bultmann and Tillich, and even hail the oracular but vacuous abstractions of Bultmann's letter to the Sheffield Industrial Mission, setting out his 'demythologized' version of the Gospel, as an example of 'profound simplicity'.[1] Indeed, analysis shows that the modern 'broad church', liberal, and existentialist positions, however superficially different, are all really members of the same

[1] *Honest to God*, p. 25; text of letter in ed. D. A. Edwards: *The Honest to God Debate* (London, 1963), pp. 138f.

theological family. They are all versions of what we may call Renaissance theology, the Erasmian type of thought within Protestantism. Renaissance theology is characteristically rationalistic, anti-dogmatic, and agnostic in temper, ethical and humanitarian in its interests, and ready to hail almost any kind of religious outlook and belief about God (and the Bishop of Woolwich adds in certain types of atheism too) as having in it the substance of Christian faith, so long as it recognizes the absoluteness of Christian moral values. Between, on the one hand, Renaissance theology and, on the other, the Reformed and 'Catholic' traditions, which agree at least in holding that Christian faith involves believing the Creed, so great a gulf is fixed that both evangelicals and 'catholics' often find themselves unable to treat teaching of the Renaissance type as Christian at all. Certainly, as both these schools within the Church of England stressed a century ago, when faced with *Essays and Reviews*, and as both have stressed again more recently in face of *Honest to God*, our formularies make it impossible to regard any type of Renaissance theology as other than a cuckoo in the Anglican nest.

Of all these varieties of Renaissance theology, and with them the cross-bred 'dialectical theology', which has one foot in the Reformation camp and the other in the Renaissance camp, and shifts its weight from foot to foot according to who expounds it, three things have to be said. First, these positions are all *subjectivist* in character – that is, they all depend on denying at some point the correlation between Scripture and faith, biblical revelation and inward illumination, the Spirit in the Scriptures and the Spirit in the heart, and on appealing to the latter to justify forsaking the former. In other words, one only reaches them by backing at some point one's private view of what the Bible is, or should be, driving at against what it actually says, and jettisoning in practice part of what it teaches in order to maintain this private opinion. In principle and method, these subjectivist positions all part company with both Reformation and 'Catholic' theology to line up with the sixteenth-century Anabaptists and seventeenth-century Quakers, who held that the 'internal word' or 'inner light' justified them in sitting loose to 'God's Word written'.

Second, these positions are all *unstable*, for they recognize no objective criterion of truth, nor method for establishing it, save the more or less speculative reasoning of individual

65

theologians, whose conclusions never command full agreement within their own camp, let alone outside it. The pendulum keeps swinging all the time; systems rise and fall; theological fashions, like fashions in the styling of cars or ladies' hats, rapidly come and go. The first quarter of this century was the age of liberalism, dominated by Harnack; the second quarter was the age of dialecticism, dominated by Barth; the third quarter seems to be the age of existentialism, dominated by Bultmann and Tillich; the fourth quarter, if the Lord tarries, will no doubt see the rise of some other fashionable 'ism', and be dominated by somebody else. The truth is that the world of Renaissance theology is a desert of continually shifting sand, where stability is impossible. Listening to the babel of Renaissance theologians' voices, confident though they often are, one soon sees that there is no hope of reaching certainty about anything in such company. Relativism is the ruling principle; every question goes back again and again into the melting-pot; syntheses are merely provisional, and the state of flux is never-ending.

Third, so far as they fail to uphold the authority of the Spirit in the Scriptures over the Spirit in the theologian, and deviate from the task of expounding and applying what the Bible actually says, these positions are really *sub-Christian*; as the rest of this chapter will show.

GOD-BREATHED SCRIPTURE

We come now to state in outline what we take to be the true view, as it is certainly the historic Anglican view, of the Holy Scriptures. Traditionally, it has been summed up by calling the Bible, as in the marriage service, 'God's Word', or, as in Article XX, 'God's Word written'. The value of such phraseology is that it at once indicates, first, that what Scripture says, God says (the Word *of God*); second, that the Scriptures together make up a total presentation of God's message to men (*the* Word of God); third, that the Scriptures constitute a message addressed directly by God to everyone who reads or hears them (the *Word* of God) – in other words, that the Scriptures have the nature of *preaching*. The 'Word of the Lord' conveyed by the prophets in their oracles, and the 'Word of God' set forth by the apostles in their sermons, was always a word applying directly to its hearers, summoning them to

66

recognize that God Himself was thereby addressing them, calling on them to respond to His instruction and direction, and working in them through God's own Spirit to evoke the response which it required (cf. I Thess. 2:13). Similarly, the Bible as a whole, viewed from the standpoint of its contents, should be thought of, not statically, but dynamically; not merely as what God said long ago, but as what He says still; and not merely as what He says to men in general, but as what He says to each individual reader or hearer in particular. In other words, Holy Scripture should be thought of as *God preaching* — God preaching to me every time I read or hear any part of it — God the Father preaching God the Son in the power of God the Holy Ghost. God the Father is the giver of Holy Scripture; God the Son is the theme of Holy Scripture; and God the Spirit, as the Father's appointed agent in witnessing to the Son, is the author, authenticator, and interpreter, of Holy Scripture. This is the position which we shall now try to elucidate, by means of some further study of what biblical inspiration implies.

We saw in the last chapter what inspiration was in the prophets: a divine work, taking many psychological forms, whereby, having made God's message known to them, the Holy Spirit so overruled all their subsequent mental activity in giving the message poetic and literary form that each resultant oracle was as truly a divine utterance as a human, as direct a disclosure of what was in God's mind as of what was in the prophet's. Also, we saw that the New Testament extends this concept of dual authorship to cover all the Old Testament, second-person psalms of address to God (cf. Heb. 1:8–12, 2:6ff.) or admonitions from the wise man to his pupil (cf. Heb. 12:5f.), and third-person narratives of God's words and doings, as well as first-person divine utterances spoken through prophetic messengers. Our Lord quotes the narrator's marginal comment in Genesis 2:24 as what 'he which made them . . . said' (Mt. 19:4f.). Paul tells the Corinthian Christians that the history of Israel's wilderness wanderings was 'written for our admonition, upon whom the ends of the ages are come' (I Cor. 10:10; cf. Rom. 15:4). Paul also calls the Old Testament as a whole 'the oracles of God' (Rom. 3:2; cf. Acts 7:38), and twice says 'Scripture' when he means 'God, as recorded in Scripture' ('the Scripture, foreseeing . . . preached . . .' [Gal. 3:2]; 'the Scripture saith unto Pharaoh, For this very

67

purpose did I raise thee up' [Rom. 9:17]). Thus he shows that for him biblical statements were, quite simply, words of God talking about Himself. Similarly, in Romans 4 and Galatians 3:6ff., Paul treats what 'the Scripture saith' about Abraham (that he 'believed God, and it was counted unto him for righteousness') as divine testimony to the way of salvation. The New Testament concept of Old Testament inspiration is crystallized in the statement in II Timothy 3:16, 'all Scripture is inspired by God' (R.S.V.), where 'inspired by God' is *theopneustos*, literally 'breathed out from God'. The thought here is that, just as God made the host of heaven 'by the breath of his mouth' (Ps. 33:6), through His own creative fiat, so we should regard the Scriptures as the product of a similar creative fiat – 'let there be Law, Prophets, and Writings' (the three divisions of the Jewish canon in New Testament times). The New Testament faith about the Old Testament was that the real narrator of Israel's history in the Law and Former Prophets (that is, the Pentateuch and historical books), and the real psalmist, poet, and wisdom-teacher in the Writings, as well as the real preacher of the prophets' sermons, was God Himself.

Moreover, we have also seen that our Lord, according to His own explicit testimony, spoke from God, and so did His apostles, to whom He promised His Spirit to enable them to do precisely this in their witness to Himself (see Jn. 14:26, 15:26f., 16:7–15, 20:21ff.; cf. Mt. 10:19f.; Lk. 10:16; I Cor. 2:12f.). Apostolic witness to Christ, spoken or written, thus has the same Spirit-prompted, divine-human character – that is, is inspired in the same sense – as the sacred books of the Old Testament. As, therefore, we should follow the New Testament Christians in viewing the Old Testament as given by God for our learning, so we should read the New Testament as part of Jesus Christ's legacy to us – as if at each point we heard Him say, 'I had Paul (or John, or Matthew, or whoever it is) write this in order to help *you*'. This is what it means to believe in biblical inspiration biblically.

The inspiring process, which brought each writer's thoughts into such exact coincidence with those of God, necessarily involved a unique oversight and control of those who were its subjects. Some moderns doubt whether this control could leave room for any free mental activity on the writers' part, and pose a dilemma: *either* God's control of the writers was complete, in which case they wrote as robots or automata (which clearly they did not), *or* their minds worked freely as they wrote the Scriptures, in which case God could not fully have controlled them, or kept them from error. Exponents of this dilemma usually hold that the evidence for errors (false statements purporting to be true) in the Bible is in fact as conclusive as the evidence for spontaneous self-expression by its human writers. But our first comment must be that this is not so. That Scripture errs has been assumed by many, but it cannot in principle be proved, any more than it can be proved that Jesus was not morally perfect. Both questions are actually settled farther back: if Jesus was God incarnate, He could not but be morally perfect, and if Scripture is the Word of the God of truth it cannot but be true and trustworthy at all points. Moreover, the dilemma rests on the assumption that full psychological freedom of thought and action, and full subjection to divine control, are incompatible; and this is not true either. If the inspiration of the prophets was what all Scripture says it was, it is absurd to deny that the whole Bible could be similarly inspired.

Instead of imposing on God arbitrary limitations of this sort, we should rather adore the wisdom and power that could so order the unruly minds of sinful men as to cause them freely and spontaneously, with no inhibiting of their normal mental processes, to write only and wholly the infallible truth of God. As B. B. Warfield observed, we are not to imagine that when God wanted Paul's letters written 'He was reduced to the necessity of going down to the earth and painfully scrutinizing the men He found there, seeking anxiously for the one who, on the whole, promised best for His purpose; and then violently forcing the material he wished expressed through him, against his natural bent, and with as little loss from his recalcitrant characteristics as possible. Of course, nothing of the sort took place. If God wished to give His people a series of letters like Paul's, He prepared a Paul to write them, and the Paul He brought to the task was a Paul who spontaneously would write just such letters.'[1] Of course – but what a marvel of providential management this was! And, for that matter, what a marvel of condescending mercy it was that God should speak to men at all! And what patience and skill He showed throughout the

[1] B. B. Warfield: *The Inspiration and Authority of the Bible* (London, 1951), p. 155.

69

long history of revelation in always so adapting His message to the capacities of His chosen messengers that it never overran their powers of transmission, but within the limits set by their mind, outlook, culture, language, and literary ability, could always find adequate and exact expression! But such gracious self-limitation is typical of the God of Bethlehem's stable and Calvary's cross.

Inspiration took many psychological forms; here, as elsewhere, God showed Himself a God of variety. The basic form of the process was *dualistic* inspiration, in which the recipient of revelation remained conscious throughout of the distinction between himself, the hearer and reporter, and God, the Speaker to and through him. The inspiration that produced the Old Testament prophetic oracles, including the Mosaic legislation, and the apocalyptic visions of Daniel and John the divine, was of this kind. But there were other forms, too, in which this consciousness was not present, so that the human authors may well not have been aware of being inspired, in the strict sense of the word, at all. There was, on the one hand, *lyric* inspiration, in which the inspiring action of God was fused with the concentrating, intensifying, and shaping mental processes of what, in the secular sense, we would call the inspiration of the poet. This produced the Psalms, the lyrical drama of Job (which as it stands is a highly-wrought theological poem, whatever basis it may be thought to have in historical fact), the Song of Solomon, and the many great prayers that we find scattered through the historical books. Then, on the other hand, there were various forms of *organic* inspiration, whereby the inspiring action of God coalesced with the mental processes – inquiring, analytical, reflective, interpretative, applicatory – of the teacher, seeking to distil and pass on knowledge of facts and right thoughts about them. This type of inspiration produced the historical books of both Testaments, the apostolic letters, and, in the Old Testament, the books of Proverbs and Ecclesiastes. There was, of course, nothing to prevent the same man being the medium at different times of different forms of divine inspiration, and it seems clear that all three were combined in the highest degree in the inspiration of our Lord Himself. The importance of these observations lies in the fact that to recognize what form of inspiration each biblical passage displays is always the first essential for interpreting it soundly.

We are now in a position to take up the vexed issue of the authority of Scripture. Authority, the right to rule, belongs ultimately to God the Creator, and Christianity is ultimately a matter of bowing to His authority by obedient response to His revelation. On this formula all Christians agree. All, therefore, acknowledge Scripture, the written record of God's revelation, as in some sense authoritative for faith and life. But when we ask, in what sense, agreement ends, and conflicts begin. A clear grasp, however, of the meaning of biblical inspiration, as set forth above, will go far to guide us through these tangles of controversy.

The first problem that arises concerns *the nature of biblical authority*. Liberal Protestants, viewing the Bible as no more than fallible human witness to the revelatory process, and doubtful whether that process really involved divine speech to man, or whether any Scripture statements can be taken as actual utterances of God, build their concept of biblical authority in terms of three thoughts: first, the necessity of the Bible, as the only source of knowledge about God's revelatory acts; second, the quality of the Bible, as a testament of deep religious experience; third, the potency of the Bible, proved down the centuries, to bring moral and spiritual uplift to all sorts and conditions of men. On this basis, as is plain, questions like: did all the things which Scripture records happen as recorded?, did the biblical writers' thoughts express true insight at every point?, can every part of the Bible yield genuine instruction and guidance today?, still remain open, and it is in fact assumed from the start that, the Bible being, for all its religious and theological expertise, a merely human book, the answer to all three questions is probably no. This approach makes the theologian appear, willy-nilly, as a sort of salvage man, using the criteria of modern mental culture to pick out what is of value from the mass of miscellaneous antique matter that the Bible contains. Also, it puts him on the defensive, making him hesitant and apologetic whenever, following Scripture, he ventures to affirm the supernatural, as if he expects every minute to be told by a colleague that the items he has selected from the mass are not really worth much. The substance of the common liberal complaint that conservative evangelicals give too little place to reason in formulating the doctrine of authority seems only to be a feeling of injury and offence that evangelicals do not approach these questions with the same negative presuppositions, nor show the same deference to the axioms and attitudes of unbelief.

But this whole approach is incorrect, for it views biblical authority in purely human, relative terms, whereas in fact, as the doctrine of inspiration makes plain, the authority of Scripture is the divine authority of God Himself speaking. The Bible is not only man's word, but God's also; not merely a record of revelation, but a written revelation in its own right, God's own witness to Himself in the form of human witness to Him. Accordingly, the authority of the Scriptures rests, not simply on their worth as an historical source, a testament of religion, and a means of uplift, real though this is, but primarily and essentially on the fact that they come to us from the mouth of God. Therefore the real task for reason in this connection is not to try to censure and correct the Scriptures, but rather, with God's help, to try to understand and apply them, so that God may effectively censure and correct us.

But, it is objected, does not the Christian stand directly under the authority of the Lord Jesus Christ, and is not Jesus Christ Lord also of the Scriptures? And if so, how can the Christian be said to be bound to the authority of the Bible? The answer is very simple. The antithesis is a false one. Jesus Christ is Lord of the Scriptures in the same sense in which any absolute monarch is Lord of the laws and proclamations which he sees fit to issue for the government of his subjects. The ruler's laws carry his personal authority, and the measure of one's loyalty to him is the consistency of one's observance of them. But Holy Scripture, 'the sceptre of God', as Calvin calls it, is Christ's instrument of government: it comes to us, so to speak, from His hand and with His seal upon it, for He Himself commended the Old Testament to us as having His Father's authority,[1] and He Himself authorized and em-

---

[1] See, for proof of this, and discussion of the passages in Christ's teaching which some take as showing His rejection of Old Testament authority, J. W. Wenham: *Our Lord's View of the Old Testament* (London, 1953), especially pp. 28ff.; R. V. G. Tasker: *Our Lord's Use of the Old Testament* (London, 1953; = Chapter II of *The Old Testament in the New Testament*: 2nd. ed., London, 1954); N. B. Stonehouse: *The Witness of Matthew and Mark to Christ* (Philadelphia, 1944); J. I. Packer: *Our Lord's Understanding of the Law of God* (London, 1962).

72

powered the apostles to speak in His name, by His Spirit and with His own authority.[1] So the way to bow to the authority of Jesus Christ is precisely by bowing to the authority of the inspired Scriptures.

BIBLICAL INTERPRETATION

But a second problem now arises. Granted that biblical teaching, because it is divine teaching, must be our rule of faith and life, *how are we to interpret the Bible* and extract its teaching from it?

We cannot here answer this question as it deserves, for that would take a book; what we can do, however, is to show that the guiding principles for interpreting Scripture all follow from the doctrine of inspiration.

Interpretation, says J. D. Wood, is 'the way of reading an ancient book in order that it may become relevant to the life and thought of a later day'.[2] If the Bible is the divine-human product we take it to be, then the interpreting of it involves three distinct activities: *exegesis, synthesis,* and *application.* We will say a word about each.

Because the Bible is a human book, God having chosen to convey His teaching to us in the form of the inspired instruction of His human penmen, the way into His mind is necessarily *via* their minds. So the basic discipline in biblical interpretation must always be exegetical analysis – that is, the attempt to determine as exactly as possible just what the writer meant by the words he wrote, and how he would explain the sense of his statements could we cross-question him about them. Exegesis involves, on the one hand, setting each passage against its external background (historical, cultural, geographical, linguistic, literary), and, on the other hand, determining from its intrinsic characteristics its aim, scope, standpoint, presuppositions, and range and limit of interest. The first part of this task may call for a good deal of technical learning, but this does not mean that exegesis is work for scholars only; the decisive part of the task is the second part, for which the first is, at most, only ground-clearing, and in this the professional scholar does not stand on any higher footing than any diligent

[1] See N. Geldenhuys: *Supreme Authority* (London, 1953), especially pp. 45ff.
[2] J. D. Wood: *The Interpretation of the Bible* (London, 1958), pp. 1f.

student of the text in any language. The supreme requirement for understanding a biblical book – or, indeed, any other human document – is sympathy with its subject-matter, and a mind and heart that can spontaneously enter into the author's outlook. But the capacity to put oneself in the shoes of Isaiah, or Paul, or John, and see with his eyes and feel with his heart is the gift, not of academic training, but of the Holy Ghost through the new birth.

To take the measure of the mind of each biblical prophet, apostle, historian, psalmist, and wisdom writer, might seem work enough in itself; but in fact exegetical analysis is only the beginning of the interpretative task. Because the Bible is a divine book as well as a human one, and because the sixty-six separate documents that make it up, under all their human diversity, are products of a single divine mind setting forth a single message, it is necessary to proceed from exegesis to synthesis, and to seek to integrate the fruits of our study of the individual books and writers into a single coherent whole. We come to the task of exegesis with the knowledge that all the human author's thoughts concerning God are God's own thoughts too; but when we move on to the further task of synthesis, we soon become aware that at point after point God's thoughts go further and embrace more than those of any one biblical writer did or could. The full significance of each passage only appears when it is set in the context of all the rest of Scripture – which its own author, of course, was never able to do. The Bible appears like a symphony orchestra, with the Holy Ghost as its Toscanini; each instrumentalist has been brought willingly, spontaneously, creatively, to play his notes just as the great conductor desired, though none of them could ever hear the music as a whole. Not only the prophets who foretold Christ (cf. I Pet. 1: 10–12), but all the writers of both Testaments, are constantly telling us more than ever they themselves knew. The point of each part only becomes fully clear when seen in relation to all the rest.

In this task of synthesis, the guiding principle must be the self-consistency of Scripture, in other words the principle, that in giving us the Bible the Holy Ghost did not contradict Himself-consistency of Scripture, in other words the principle that As they understood it, it was really three principles in one. It was, first, the principle of working from the centre outwards, explaining what is secondary by the light of what is primary,

74

and what is obscure in terms of what is clear. This in practice meant – and means – recognizing that the central themes of the Bible are the kingdom, people, and covenant of God, and the person, place, work, and glory, of the Lord Jesus Christ – in other words, as Luther pregnantly put it, the law and the Gospel. Second, the Reformers' phrase signified the principle of following out the inner links of Scripture. This meant, for instance, understanding Old Testament prophecy in the light of the New Testament account of its fulfilment, understanding types in the light of their antitypes, understanding Leviticus in the light of Hebrews, and the doings of Old Testament characters in the light of New Testament comment on them. Third, 'the analogy of faith' meant the principle of understanding Scripture harmonistically, not setting text against text or supposing apparent contradictions to be real ones, but seeking rather to let one passage throw light on another, in the certainty that there is in Scripture a perfect agreement between part and part, which careful study will be able to bring out. The Articles apply this principle twice. With our Lord (Jn. 5:39, 46), Paul (Rom. 4), and the writer to the Hebrews (*passim*), and against sixteenth-century Anabaptists and, along with them, earlier Marcionites and later liberals and dispensationalists, Article VII affirms that 'the Old Testament is not contrary to the New; for both in the Old and New Testament everlasting life is offered to Mankind through Christ . . .' Also, Article XX states that, 'although the (visible) Church be a witness and a keeper of holy Writ,' it may not 'so expound one place of Scripture, that it be repugnant to another' – for such exposition must be wrong.

So, then, to take one example, it would not be right to dismiss the imprecatory Psalms in the way that many do, as vindictive outbursts contrary to the mind of God, expressing the vengeful spirit which the New Testament condemns. The Homilies themselves warn us against this mistake. The truth is that what Psalms like 35, 58, 109, and 137:7–9 are voicing is a zeal and passion for God's glory, and for the triumph of His cause and His righteousness, which far exceeds ours, in the same way that Psalms 17:1–5, 26:1–5, and 131 express a humility and simplicity of spirit that is far above our own. Just as, had we written the words of these latter Psalms, they would have argued priggishness and conceit, and the words of triumph-songs like Judges 5, Isaiah 47 and Revelation 19:1–3, had they been our words, would have savoured of gloating, so too the words of the cursing Psalms, had we spoken them, would have revealed an all-too-human ill-will. But this only means that our hearts are less pure than the hearts of the psalmists. David, writes the homilist, 'spake them (the imprecations) not of a private hatred, and in a stomach against their persons; but wished spiritually the destruction of such corrupt errors and vices, which reigned in all devilish persons set against God . . . he hated the wicked . . . with a perfect hate (Ps. 139: 21f.), not with a malicious hate to the hurt of the soul. Which perfection of spirit, because it cannot be performed in us, so corrupted in affections as we be, we ought not to use in our private causes the like form in words, for that we cannot fulfil the like words in sense . . .' ('An Information for them which take Offence at certain places of the Holy Scripture': *The Homilies*, pp. 382f.). Thus the truth is that here, no less than at other points, the psalmist is expressing true devotion at its highest pitch, and the fancied disharmony between his words and New Testament ideals does not exist. In fact, the same spirit is voiced in the New Testament also: see Rev. 6: 10. Therefore the attitude of those who decline to use these verses from God's hymn-book in public worship seems doubtfully wise. Is it not good for us to be shown, even if we can hardly at present grasp, what true zeal for God's honour is like?[1]

The third part of the work of interpretation is to apply biblical teaching to ourselves, individually and corporately. It

[1] A. Kuyper observes that the standpoint of the inspired poets who wrote these Psalms was that of ultimate spiritual reality, where distinctions are absolute and 'everything that sides with God lives and has our love, and everything that chooses eternally against God bears the mark of death and rouses our hatred'. This is the standpoint that we shall all occupy in heaven, though we cannot consistently attain to it here. Seeing things from this standpoint, says Kuyper, 'the rule, "Do not I hate them, O Lord, that hate thee?" becomes the only applicable standard, and whatever departs from this rule, falls short of love for God . . . (the imprecations) are solemnly true and holy when you take your stand in the absolute palingenesis (i.e., the order of new creation, eschatologically viewed), where God's honour is the keynote of the harmony of the human heart' (*Principles of Sacred Theology* [Grand Rapids, 1954], p. 524). It will help us progressively to appropriate these Psalms and enter into their outlook if we learn to use them as prayers against Satan and his hosts, and against our own besetting sins. Cf. C. S. Lewis: *Reflections on the Psalms* (London, 1961 ed.), pp. 113f.

is here most of all that we need the help of the Spirit, who inspired the Scriptures, to give us understanding. God-inspired Scripture, writes Paul, 'is profitable for teaching, for reproof, for correction, for instruction in righteousness' (II Tim. 3 : 16); but we cannot reap this profit till the Spirit quickens our minds and consciences to measure and judge ourselves by Scripture, and to discern the issues of repentance, and faith, and obedience, and amending of our ways, which across the centuries Holy Scripture forces upon us. Here, again, the decisive qualification is not academic scholarship, but rather a praying, humble, teachable heart. The rule that applies is that to him that hath shall be given: it is only as we obey God up to the limit of our present insight into His will that our insight will be deepened and our vision enlarged. Live by the light you have as to the bearing of Scripture on your life, and you shall have more light; neglect the light you have, and you will actually darken it, so that in the outcome you will have less. This solemn alternative faces every Christian every day of his life.

It is obvious that in practice all three parts of the task of biblical interpretation will, and must, be carried on together, and that deepened insight at any one stage will result in deeper insight at the other two stages also. It is obvious too that the enterprise may break down at any of its three stages. It seems clear that in present-day Protestantism it has largely broken down at all three stages. Unwillingness to take seriously the biblical writers' thoughts as being, strictly and precisely, the communicated thoughts of God; unwillingness to be led and bound by the analogy of faith in unifying the fruits of exegesis; and indolence in seeking to apply to human life what the Bible actually says – these are the root causes of our 'famine of hearing the words of the Lord'. And there is no hope of the famine being alleviated till these things are penitently put right.

THE SUFFICIENCY OF SCRIPTURE

What we have said so far in this chapter might well lower our stock in the eyes of many liberal and 'broad church' Anglicans, but would, we think, command the substantial assent of most Anglo-Catholics, and with them members of the Roman and Orthodox communions too. But now we come to the third problem in connection with biblical authority, the question of *the sufficiency of Scripture*, and here we reach the second great parting of the ways in connection with our view of the Bible.[1] The so-called 'Catholic' (as opposed to 'Reformed') tradition, in all its forms, holds that Holy Scripture, interpreted in terms of itself, is not sufficient as a guide for those who would live under the authority of God. Church tradition is necessary (it is said) to lead us into the right understanding of the Scriptures, which is not accessible from a straightforward study of the text. True, holders of this position disagree among themselves as to what 'Church tradition' is. The Roman Council of Trent spoke of unwritten apostolic traditions, passed on orally in the Church down the ages, as being a second source of doctrine alongside the Scriptures – a fact which embarrasses many modern Roman theologians, who prefer to work with a dynamic, 'open-ended' concept of tradition as the word of God in the hearts of the (Roman) faithful, constantly crystallizing out through the Spirit's stimulus into consensus of opinion which is then at point after point infallibly recorded in successive papal definitions. Anglo-Catholic and Orthodox teachers, by contrast, make use of an organic, but circumscribed, idea of tradition as, in general, the developed faith and outlook of the universal Church during the first centuries of its life and, in particular, its sacraments, creeds, Scriptures, and ministers, and its convictions about each. Detailed differences between these groups spring directly from their differing views of tradition, but these need not delay us. What concerns us at present is simply the fact that 'Catholics' of every sort unite against 'Reformed' Christians in insisting that tradition is more than the Scriptures, that the Scriptures are only part of the authoritative legacy of the past that must determine our faith, and that therefore they may not be detached from the rest of tradition and set to judge it, but must themselves be construed in harmony with it; for what tradition says is what Scripture must mean, and if we take it to mean anything contrary we necessarily misunderstand it.[2]

[1] For the first, see pp. 49 ff. above.
[2] Regrettably, this principle found its way into the Committee Report on the Bible at the 1958 Lambeth Conference. 'The Anglican Communion appeals to the whole of that primitive tradition of which the Sacraments, the Creeds, the Canon of the Bible, and the historic episcopate are all parts. The New Testament is thus not to be seen in isolation: the Church preceded it in time, and it was within the

Thus, when 'Catholics' say (as in these days many of them are ready, perhaps too ready, to do) that the Bible is our authoritative rule of faith, what they mean is that our standard of truth must be the interpretation of the Bible which tradition gives us – not, even in principle, that interpretation at which one would arrive by simply comparing Scripture with Scripture. Endless confusion arises in discussion with 'Catholics', as modern ecumenical theology makes painfully apparent, when it is not seen that what they and what 'Reformed' Christians mean by biblical authority are two quite different things.

The issue here is whether Holy Scripture, as a written revelation from God, is in itself complete, clear, and decisive, as a rule for our faith and life, or not. On this question the Church of England took a firm and unambiguous stand four centuries ago. Article VI of the Thirty-Nine affirms the sufficiency of Scripture alone as a rule of faith. 'Holy Scripture containeth all things necessary to salvation; so that whatsoever is not read therein, nor may be proved thereby, is not to be required of any man, that it should be believed as an article of the Faith . . .' Article VIII follows this up by telling us that the most venerable and time-honoured products of tradition – the Apostles', Nicene, and Athanasian Creeds – are to be taken as true, not just because they are traditional, but because 'they may be proved by most certain warrants of Holy Scripture'. It is not denied that the ecumenical creeds offer themselves as a guide to the interpretation of Holy Scripture; what is denied, however, is that we may lawfully accept them in that capacity without first testing them by those very Scriptures whose substance they seek to set forth. For the creeds, like the decisions of all popes, councils, and individual churches (see Articles XIX, XXI), are the work of sinful men, to whom no personal infallibility was ever promised; therefore they must be verified by appeal to what the homilist calls God's 'infallible Word' (*The Homilies*, p. 383), and not treated as themselves an 'infallible word' which should control our interpretation of Scripture. The presupposition of our formularies is that Holy Scripture, interpreted from within itself in the manner which we have described, by means of grammatico-historical exegesis and the analogy of faith, constitutes a clear, definite, and

Church, with its Sacraments, Creeds, and Apostolic Ministry, that the New Testament was canonized' (*The Lambeth Conference 1958, 2,* 4).

obligatory rule of faith and life, by which all belief and behaviour, corporate and private, must be directed, and to which all controversies between Christians must be brought for settlement.

Such is the historic Anglican position: is it the right one? Unquestionably it is. It rests on two principles. The first is that all Christians of all ages must align themselves with the churches of New Testament times in direct subjection to the doctrinal and practical teaching of the apostles. The apostles were God's chosen and anointed witnesses to Christ (cf. Acts 1:8, 10:39–43). Their teaching, organically linked with the Old Testament, the fulfilment of which they announced, was truth from God, revealed and inspired by Christ's Spirit and set forth in His name and with His authority. As such it forms an authoritative standard of truth and criterion of error, not only for the apostles' own time, but for all time. We find Paul and Peter and John all insisting that hearty acceptance of the teaching they had given, and submission to its authority, is a basic test of true spirituality and godliness, not to mention fitness for the ministry (I Cor. 14:37; II Cor. 11:3f., 13:2-10; Gal. 1:6–9; I Thess. 1:5, 2:13; II Thess. 2:13–15, 3:6–15; II Tim. 2:1f., 3:13f.; Tit. 1:9; II Pet. 1:12–2:3; I Jn. 2:21–24, 4:6; II Jn. 9f.). Were they back among us today, they would still say the same – perhaps even more emphatically! To throw over the authority of apostolic teaching in any degree is, to that extent, a lapse from Christianity. This is the first principle. The second is simply the incontrovertible fact that, as E. A. Litton puts it, 'no apostolical teaching is certainly extant except that which is embalmed in the New Testament'.[1] Hence it follows that the apostolic New Testament, read in conjunction with the Old, of which it is the completion, must always be our final authority and court of appeal. Christ's Church was, and is, to be ruled by His apostles; therefore, by their providentially surviving writings. To say that Christ must be allowed to rule, that the Redeemer must be given His crown rights, is thus to say that Scripture must be allowed to rule, that the Bible must always have the last word.

[1] E. A. Litton: *Introduction to Dogmatic Theology* (London, 1960 ed.), pp. 30f.

To turn the flank of this argument, Roman Catholics (not to mention certain Anglicans) are accustomed to argue that the authority of the post-apostolic Church as an on-going, living, Spirit-indwelt community must be prior and superior to that of the New Testament, inasmuch as it was the post-apostolic Church that established the New Testament as a 'canon' – that is, a yardstick – of orthodox faith. But this argument fails. The Church no more gave us the New Testament canon than Sir Isaac Newton gave us the force of gravity. God gave us gravity, by His work of creation, and similarly He gave us the New Testament canon, by inspiring the individual books that make it up. Newton did not create gravity, but recognized it, by considering (so it is said) the fall of an apple; similarly, the various churches of Christendom, through a gradual, un-co-ordinated, seemingly haphazard and erratic process covering several centuries, came to recognize the extent and limits of the God-given canon, by checking and cross-checking the pedigree of the many books that bore apostolic names, or were alleged to proceed from the apostolic circle, to find out which of them could make good their claim to apostolic authorship or sanction. Had one suggested to Christians of the second, third, or fourth century that by this means the Church was creating a canon for itself, choosing out some good-quality Christian literature to authorize as a standard of faith for the future, they would have shaken their heads and marvelled that anyone could dream up an idea so perverse and far from the truth. The belief that apostolic writings, as such, were inspired, and therefore intrinsically authoritative, was the presupposition of their whole inquiry. All that the churches were trying to do was to see which of the books claiming to be in some sufficient sense apostolic really were so – a question essentially of historical fact, though one on which character and content were also held to bear, both positively and negatively.[1]

[1] For more details on the formation of the New Testament canon, and the principles involved in it, see Herman Ridderbos: 'The Canon of the New Testament' in ed. C. F. H. Henry: *Revelation and the Bible* (Grand Rapids and London, 1958), pp. 187ff.; 'Canon of the New Testament' in *The New Bible Dictionary*. The statement in Article VI that the books of the New Testament 'as they are commonly received' are those 'of whose authority was never any doubt in the Church' is a little too loose to be quite clear. The meaning apparently

After three centuries of inquiry, the greater part of Christendom was found to be agreed on its answer to this question, and its agreement was duly recorded by individual theologians and various conciliar decisions (though no conciliar decision, be it noted, was made at any stage to bring agreement into being). Good as the reasons certainly are for thinking that the Spirit, here as elsewhere, had led the Church to a correct discernment, the fact of having been guided to see which books have intrinsic authority can no more be held to give the Church authority over them, to limit their meaning to that which accords with its own tradition, than the fact of my having recognized what came in the post this morning as a genuine bookseller's bill, made out to me, gives me authority over it, to pay only so much of it as I feel inclined to.

We need to be clear that the continuing controversies between 'Reformed' and 'Catholic' Christians over such matters as the priesthood of the clergy, the apostolic succession, the authority of the episcopate, the infallibility of the pope, transubstantiation and the 'real presence', the mass-sacrifice, purgatory, indulgences, mariolatry, and the nature and number of the sacraments, cannot in principle be settled until both sides agree that the appeal to Scripture, interpreted in terms of itself – in this sense, *sola Scriptura*, Scripture *alone* – is final.

CHAPTER FIVE

GOD'S WORD HEARD

GOD has spoken, says the Bible; and godliness means *hearing His word*. 'Hearing' in this phrase means more, of course, than just being within earshot while the message of God is read aloud or recited or explained. 'Hear', in its full biblical sense, implies attention, assent, and application to oneself of the things learned; it means listening with a firm purpose to obey,

---

is that the authenticity and authority of these books was never doubted, not by individual theologians and congregations (the framers of the Articles were well aware that such a statement, if made, would be false), but by the catholic visible Church as a whole. So understood, the statement, so far as the available evidence goes, would seem to be true.

and then doing as God's Word proves to require. It is in this sense that we use the verb throughout this chapter.

What does it mean to hear God's Word? According to Hebrews, it means, quite concretely, receiving and responding to God's propositional Word (that is, His message) which He has spoken to us from heaven through the lips of His personal Word (that is, His Son), also through the utterances of prophets and apostles, concerning the 'great salvation' which the Son of God won for us by the shedding of His blood for our sins (see Heb. 1:1f., 2:3, 12:25, etc.). God's personal Word appears as the central subject of His propositional Word, both when spoken and as written. What Jesus said of the Scriptures of the Old Testament – 'these are they which bear witness of me' (Jn. 5:39) – can be said of both Testaments with equal truth. To hear 'God's Word written', therefore, means, in the last analysis, doing as God commanded at the transfiguration, when He said, 'This is my beloved Son: hear ye *him*' (Mk. 9:7); which in its turn means, not just accepting Jesus' moral teaching, but receiving Him as one's living Saviour, relying on His shed blood for the pardon of one's sins, and living henceforth as His bondslave – one of those who 'follow the Lamb whithersoever he goeth' (Rev. 14:4). The homilist reminds us that the living Christ 'speaketh presently unto us in the Holy Scriptures' (*The Homilies*, p. 370f.), and godliness means responding directly to His appeal in repentance, and faith, and discipleship. 'I heard the voice of Jesus say, "Come unto me and rest" . . . I came to Jesus . . .' Nobody who is a stranger to godliness, in this fundamental Christian sense, can be held to have heard God's Word as yet.

Three aspects of the life of godliness, viewed as a life of hearing God's word, call for particular mention.

PROMISE

Firstly, it is a life of *faith in God's promises*. Faith in the Bible is not, as existentialists make out, a leap in the dark, but rather a step in the light, whereby (to extend the metaphor) one puts one's whole weight on the firm ground of God's unshakeable promises. Paul points to Abraham as the great exemplar of faith because, when God promised him, as a childless old man of seventy-five, a host of descendants, he believed the promise, and went on believing it through thick and thin, till it began to be fulfilled in the birth of Isaac, no less than a quarter of a century later. 'Without being weakened in faith he considered his own body now as good as dead (he being about a hundred years old), and the deadness of Sarah's womb: yea, looking unto the promise of God, he wavered not through unbelief, but waxed strong through faith, giving glory to God, and being fully assured that, what he had promised, he was able also to perform. Wherefore also it was reckoned unto him for righteousness' (Rom. 4: 19–22, alluding to the recorded witness to Abraham's justification in Gen. 15: 6). Paul's immediate point is that the faith which justifies us is like that – a trust in God on the basis of His incredible-sounding assurance that He gave His Son to die, and then raised Him from death, for the express purpose of putting away our sins (verses 23f.). But this is not the only connection in which Paul's analysis of faith applies. The truth is that all faith, at every stage in our Christian pilgrimage, is essentially a resting upon God's promise. It has the nature of assurance, because it relies on God's assurances. This comes out very clearly in Hebrews 11, where faith (that which 'gives substance to our hopes, and makes us certain of realities we do not see' [verse 1, *N.E.B.*]) is depicted throughout as a spirit of obedience to God's commands on the basis of trust in His promises, both general (the promise of reward [verse 6]) and particular (such as the promise of a child to Sarah, who 'counted him faithful that had promised' [verse 11]).

The heart of the life of faith is in fact the recognition that all the promises which God is recorded as having made to His people in the past are still in principle (not always, of course, in detail, because of differing circumstances) extended to each individual Christian in the present. Faith, we may venture to say, rests upon the theology of the promise-box. This appears from Hebrews 13: 5f., where the writer teaches his readers to take to themselves God's promise to Joshua, 'I will in no wise fail thee, neither will I in any wise forsake thee' (Josh 1: 5), as a basis for their own confidence and contentment in face of opposition. The true wellspring of the Christian's peace, joy, hope, and strength to endure, lies in his being able to say, with Isaac Watts,

> Engraved as in eternal brass
> The mighty promise shines;
> Nor can the powers of darkness raze
> Those everlasting lines.

His very word of grace is strong
    As that which built the skies;
The voice that rolls the stars along
    Speaks all the promises.

My hiding-place, my refuge, tower,
    And shield, art Thou, O Lord;
I firmly anchor all my hopes
    On thy unerring Word.

The comfort of knowing that every one of God's 'precious and exceeding great promises' (II Pet. 1:4) in Holy Scripture is 'yea' in Christ for me (cf. II Cor. 1:20) is as unspeakable as is the misery of not knowing this in times of hardship, loneliness, and depression. But such is the state to which those who deny the biblical doctrine of inspiration sentence themselves; for if we cannot be sure that what Scripture says, God says, we cannot be sure that He has actually made any of the promises which Scripture ascribes to Him. (Indeed if we deny that revelation is propositional, we make it quite certain that He has not. A God who uses no words cannot make any promises).

We can now see why, as a matter of observable fact, 'critical' views of the Bible have always impoverished the life of faith, and why so many of those who hold such views today either water faith down to mere morality in a context of vague optimism, or else jazz it up into a tortured existentialist leap in the dark (or, indeed, like the author of *Honest to God*, do both together). In the nature of the case, it could hardly be otherwise. But this is neither the Christian nor the Anglican way. The Prayer Book points us insistently to God's promises as the foundation for faith and hope. This emphasis is specially strong in connection with forgiveness. 'Restore thou them that are penitent; According to thy *promises* declared unto mankind in Christ Jesu our Lord' (General Confession, Morning and Evening Prayer). 'Almighty God . . . who . . . hath *promised* forgiveness . . . have mercy upon you . . .' (Absolution, holy communion service). The communion service proceeds: 'Hear what comfortable words our Saviour Christ saith unto all that truly turn to him', and when we hear them (Mt. 11:28; Jn. 3:16; followed by I Tim. 1:15; I Jn. 2:1) we find that they are simply divine promises and assurances, set forth as a basis for confidence that there is mercy even for us. Similarly, the Prayer Book teaches us to correlate our hope with God's promise, enjoining us to pray that 'we may so faithfully serve thee in this life, that we fail not finally to attain *thy heavenly promises*' (collect for Trinity XIII). Christian hope and assurance can only exist because there are specific promises from God on which to base them, promises which the Holy Spirit seals on Christians' hearts. There is urgent need to rediscover the truth that the promises of God are the ground of faith; for where professed Christians are not living in the joy of the knowledge that all God's promises are theirs, the truth is that God's Word is not being heard.

LAW

Secondly, godliness involves *obedience to God's laws*. The Anglican view of the Bible is that it is a supremely practical book, not only leading us to know God through meeting Jesus Christ, but also giving us rules and maxims for bringing the whole of our life into line with God's will. In 1540, in his Preface to that epoch-making book, the Great Bible, ordered to be set up for public reading in every church in the country, Archbishop Cranmer wrote: 'In the Scriptures be the fat pastures of the soul; therein is no venomous meat, no unwholesome thing; they be the very dainty and pure feeding. He that is ignorant, shall find there what he should learn . . . Herein may princes learn how to govern their subjects; subjects obedience . . . to their princes: husbands, how they should behave them unto their wives; how to educate their children . . .: and contrary the wives, children, and servants may know their duty to their husbands, parents, and masters. Here may all manner of persons, men, women, young, old, learned, unlearned, rich, poor, priests, laymen, lords, ladies, officers, tenants, and mean men, virgins, wives, widows, lawyers, merchants, artificers, husbandmen, and all manner of persons, of what estate or condition soever they be, may in this book learn all things what they ought to believe, what they ought to do, and what they should not do, as well concerning Almighty God, as also concerning themselves and all other.'[1] The Bible is as much a rule for life as it is a rule of faith.

[1] Cranmer: *Remains and Letters* (Parker Society: Cambridge, 1846),

But it is important to be clear as to what sort of rule for life it is. Its moral teaching is not a code of isolated externals, a Pharisaic formalism, but a connected series of principles and ideals, deriving directly from the revealed nature of God and His purpose for man, and calling for right motives as well as right types of action. The biblical law of God requires us to be persons of a certain kind, as well as to do things of a certain kind; and the biblical concept of *love* embraces both sides of the ideal. So opposing love to law, as some do, is as perverse as opposing a woman's fondness for her husband to her efforts to provide the things she knows he likes. So far from being opposed, love and law belong inseparably together. Law is needed as love's eyes; love is needed as law's heartbeat. Law without love is Pharisaism; love without law is antinomianism; both are aberrations. Our Lord showed the connection between love and law when He said: 'If ye love me, ye will keep my commandments . . . he that hath my commandments and keepeth them, he it is that loveth me' (Jn. 14:15, 21). John put it even more succinctly: 'love means following the commands of God' (II Jn. 6, *N.E.B.*). And where Christians do not constantly expose their lives to the detailed 'reproof, correction, and instruction in righteousness' of Holy Scripture (II Tim. 3:16), the truth is that God's Word is not being heard.

TRUTH

Thirdly, genuine godliness is always marked by *delight in God's truth*. Psalm 119 makes this abundantly plain. The psalmist loves God's law, rejoices to know God's mind, and holds fast, at whatever cost to himself, the truths that God has taught him. His delight in God is, among other things, a delight in God's Word. Elsewhere in Scripture, God's Word is pictured, not only as food, because it nourishes and promotes growth (I Cor. 3:2; Heb. 5:12ff.; cf. I Pet. 2:2), but also as honey, by reason of its sweetness (Ps. 19:10, 119:103; cf. Ezek. 3:3; Rev. 10:9f.). One fears that many in our churches today are strangers to this sense of the sweetness of God's truth, as they are evidently strangers to the love of the Bible which it evokes, and to the sense of duty to keep God's truth inviolate, come what may, which found expression in the firmness of our Reformers against the pope and the mass – a firmness which under Mary led many to martyrdom. Tolerance of differences on secondary doctrinal questions is doubtless an Anglican virtue, but the all-round doctrinal indifferentism which we meet so often today is a travesty of the Anglican ideal. The Anglicanism of the 1662 Prayer Book, with its hundred-verses-a-day lectionary, its monthly passage through the Psalter, its Bible-crammed daily services, and its demand that its clergy should be men of one book, is a Bible-reading, Bible-loving, Bible-believing faith. Today, however, Anglicans devote their zeal to maintaining a state of doctrinal laxity rather than a confession of biblical truth. The Thirty-Nine Articles are mocked and disregarded in those Anglican churches that still retain them, and clerical subscription to them is nowadays largely emptied of meaning. The idea that Anglican unity is 'institutional' and 'cultic' rather than confessional is hailed as a new revelation, and all thought of doctrinal discipline in Anglican churches is scouted. What a lapse this is from the Anglicanism of the Reformers! But the case is hardly better in any of the older Reformed churches; similar symptoms of the malaise of doctrinal indifferentism appear in them all. And when biblical teaching is not revered as a transcript of God's mind, and churchmen show little sign of having 'received the *love* of the truth' (II Thess. 2:10), so as to dwell on it, and prize it, and study to keep it intact (cf. II Tim. 1:13f.), and where vital gospel doctrines are allowed to be obscured in the interests of a hollow pleasantness—the thing that Paul would not let happen in Galatia and Colossae—then the truth is that God's Word is not being heard.

THE HOLY SPIRIT

But how, we ask, does God's Word actually come to be heard? In the first place, it will certainly not be heard where the Bible is not preached, studied, or read. The first need is to give the Bible its rightful place in personal and church life. But whether, even then, God's Word will be heard depends on yet a further factor: namely, our openness to the work of the Holy Spirit.

It is the promised privilege of all Christians, we are told, to be 'taught of God' (Jn. 6:45, citing Is. 54:13), and it is the Spirit of God who teaches them. The Spirit who taught all things to the apostles (Jn. 14:26, 16:13f.; I Cor. 2:10, 13) is the 'anointing' that teaches all Christ's people (I Jn. 2:27).

He teaches us not by fresh disclosures of hitherto unknown truth, like those whereby the apostles were taught, but by enabling us, who, being fallen, are by nature wholly insensitive and unresponsive to God and the things of God, to recognize the divinity, and bow to the authority, of divine realities set before us. Historically, theologians have called this work illumination, or enlightenment, or the inner witness of the Spirit. It was to this work that our Lord referred when He said that the Spirit's work would be to *convict* (Jn. 16:8). By it, the Spirit authenticates the prophetic and apostolic word to our consciences as being, in truth, what it claims to be, God's message, just as He authenticates Jesus Christ to us as being, in truth, what He claimed to be, God's Son and man's Saviour. The Spirit brings us to acknowledge the divinity claimed by, and for, Christ on the one hand, and the Scriptures on the other, as being, in truth, self-evidencing; thus He leads us to bow to the conjoint authority of both. He further enables us to grasp what both are saying to us, and works in our minds and hearts to apply the divine instruction effectively, and make us respond. It was through the Spirit's work that the Thessalonians, having 'received from us [Paul] the word of the message, even the word of God . . . accepted it not as the word of men, but, as it is in truth, the word of God'. It was also in virtue of the Spirit's action that Paul could speak of his message as a word which 'worketh in you that believe' (I Thess. 2:13).

But are we open to this working of the Spirit? As long as we approach the Scriptures with detachment, concerned only to appreciate them historically, or aesthetically, and as long as we treat them as a merely human record, we scarcely are. We are only open to the Spirit's ministry so far as we are willing, as it were, to step into the Bible, to take our stand alongside the men to whom God spoke – Abraham listening to God in Ur, Moses listening to God at Sinai, the Israelites listening to God's word from the lips of Moses and the prophets, the Jews listening to Jesus, the Romans and Corinthians and Timothy listening to Paul, and so on – and, in terms of our earlier illustration, to share joint tutorials with them, noting what God said to them and then seeking to see, in the light of that, what He would say to us. Such willingness is in most of us very limited; we are prejudiced, lazy, and unprepared for the exercise of spirit and conscience that it involves. But greater willingness and

increased receptiveness are themselves the Spirit's gifts. Therefore we must use the prayer, 'teach me thy statutes' (Ps.
119 : 12, and seven times more in this Psalm), as a plea, not
only for teaching but also for teachableness; for without the
latter we shall never have the former.

FINDING THE WORD OF THE LORD

We began this book by bringing into focus a problem, the
reality of which seems undeniable – namely, that for all the intense biblical study and detailed biblical knowledge of our day,
our churches suffer from a widespread 'famine of hearing the
words of the Lord'. We have tried to see how this came about,
and to outline as simply as we could the way of approach to the
Bible which we believe to be both right in itself, and authenti-
cally Anglican, and which, if followed, will lead us to the place
where God's Word is effectively heard once more. Readers of
this book, who, like its writer, are children of an age that is
heavily conditioned against the 'old paths' will feel that this
approach raises problems. It is no part of our concern to deny
this; we would only invite our readers to consider, in the light
of what we have said, whether alternative approaches do not
raise greater problems still. In a book of this brevity it is not
possible to consider many of the problems of which one would
have to take note in a treatise, any more than it is possible to
deal with the hundred and one problems – exegetical, historical, moral, scientific – that arise when one actually gets
down to studying and meditating on the biblical text in the
light of the principles stated. Nor, perhaps, would it have
been desirable to do so in any case. For this book is offered,
not as a treatise, but simply as a tract – a mental and spiritual
preparation and, we hope, incentive to the venture of studying
the Bible for oneself in the waiting, expectant, God-seeking,
God-fearing spirit of Samuel in the temple – 'Speak; for thy
servant heareth' (I Sam. 3 : 10). If we allow our study of the
Bible to wait upon our finding solutions to every problem that
its contents raise, we shall never get started at all. All Bible
students carry around with them all their lives a quiverful of
unsolved problems, as well as their quota of God-taught certainties. It is idle to expect to find the answer to everything
while we are in this world. What matters is that, problems not-

withstanding, we should all actually be engaged in searching the Scriptures by the light of right principles and a right method, and so daily learning of God about our sin, and about His Son.

The feeling is sometimes voiced that the sheer quantity of technical information about the Bible which scholars possess today makes Bible study harder for laymen than it used to be, by giving them so much more to master. But the assumption that one cannot study the Bible effectively without a mass of technical theological equipment is false. If the questions one brings to Scripture are such as these – 'What does this tell me about God? about myself? about my Saviour? How does this fit in with the rest of what I know of the Bible? If this is what God said to so-and-so then, what is His word to me here and now? If this is how God dealt with so-and-so in his situation, how would He deal with me in mine?' – and if one pays attention to the context and flow of thought within each book as one reads it, especially if one uses a Bible with good marginal references, God the Spirit will see to it that, layman no less than theologian, one will learn what one needs to know.

What *does* make Bible study harder for laymen nowadays than it used to be is the breakdown of the great evangelical tradition of large-scale expository preaching Sunday by Sunday from our pulpits. The New Testament pattern is that public preaching of God's Word provides, so to speak, the main meals, and constitutes the chief means of grace, and one's own personal meditations on biblical truth should come in as ancillary to this, having the nature of a series of supplementary snacks – necessary, indeed, in their place, but never intended to stand alone as a complete diet. There is something deeply unnatural and unsatisfactory in a situation where the people of God have to rely entirely on personal Bible study for their spiritual nourishment, due to lack of effective expository preaching in public worship. But this is a different issue, which we cannot pursue here.

Let it be clear, once more, that we are not belittling technical biblical scholarship. Our only point is that it is not to biblical experts alone that the Holy Ghost vouchsafes His teaching, and that the psalmist's description of the law of the Lord as 'making wise the simple' (Ps. 19 : 10) still holds good.

At the 1958 Lambeth Conference, the first committee report

dealt with 'The Holy Bible: its Authority and Message'.[1] Despite some unhappy features (its denial of the sufficiency of Scripture, noted above,[2] and of biblical inerrancy, and the inadequacy of its treatment of the biblical thought of God as speaking),[3] it contained much that was excellent, and laid specially welcome emphasis on the importance of biblical exposition in the pulpit and the reading of the Bible personally and in the home. In this, of course, it simply reaffirmed foundation-principles of Reformed Anglicanism. The Conference as a whole endorsed the report with a series of resolutions, including a call to 'all Church people to re-establish the habit of Bible-reading at home',[4] and a summons to 'the Churches of the Anglican Communion to engage in a special effort during the next ten years to extend the scope and deepen the quality of personal and corporate study of the Bible'.[5] The Encyclical Letter spoke in this connection of the clergyman's duty to work at his preaching in order to make the Bible 'come alive' to his hearers, and of 'the duty of the laity to bring to the hearing of the Bible an expectant heart, and to learn again the art of private Bible study and meditation'.[6] Admirable words—but it seems that during the six years since the Conference very little has been done in response to them.

But who among Protestants have done better? We applaud, sometimes a little patronizingly, the encouragement that the Roman hierarchy is now giving to its laity to become better acquainted with the Bible. But what a hollow gesture this is, when so many Protestant layfolk have abandoned the kind of serious Bible study, and the mass of clergy have given up the kind of serious expository preaching, that made evangelical Protestantism great and potent in days past!

'These things saith he that hath the seven Spirits of God ...; thou hast a name that thou livest and art dead. Be watchful, and strengthen the things which remain, that are ready to die.... Remember therefore how thou hast received and heard, and hold fast, and repent' (Rev. 3:1–3). May this book, despite all its gaps and limitations, help us to hear at any rate *this* word.

[1] *The Lambeth Conference 1958, 2*, 1–18.
[2] Above, p. 96 and note 10.
[3] *2*, 7.
[4] *1*, 33 (Resolution 5).
[5] *1*, 34 (Resolution 12).
[6] *1*, 19.

'God therefore, for his mercies' sake, vouchsafed to purify our minds through faith in His Son Jesus Christ, and to instil the heavenly drops of His grace into our hard stony hearts, to supple the same, that we be not contemners and deriders of His infallible Word; but that with all humbleness of mind and Christian reverence, we may endeavour ourselves to hear and to read His sacred Scriptures, and inwardly so to digest them, as shall be to the comfort of our souls, and sanctification of His holy name: to whom with the Son and the Holy Ghost, three Persons and one living God, be all laud, honour, and praise, for ever and ever. Amen' (*The Homilies*, p. 383).

O Almighty God, who by thy Son Jesus Christ didst give to Thy apostle Saint Peter many excellent gifts, and commandedst him earnestly to feed Thy flock; Make, we beseech Thee, all bishops and pastors diligently to preach Thy holy Word, and the people obediently to follow the same, that they may receive the crown of everlasting glory; through Jesus Christ our Lord. Amen (collect for Saint Peter's day).

Blessed Lord, who hast caused all holy Scriptures to be written for our learning; Grant that we may in such wise hear them, read, mark, learn, and inwardly digest them, that by patience, and comfort of Thy holy Word, we may embrace, and ever hold fast the blessed hope of everlasting life, which Thou hast given us in our Saviour Jesus Christ. Amen (collect for Advent II).

Today if ye will hear his voice, harden not your hearts: as in the provocation, and as in the day of temptation in the wilderness;

When your fathers tempted Me: proved Me, and saw My works.

Forty years long was I grieved with this generation, and said: It is a people that do err in their hearts, for they have not known My ways.

Unto whom I sware in my wrath: that they should not enter into My rest (Ps. 95: 7–11, Prayer Book version).

SUGGESTIONS FOR FURTHER READING

(*a*) Some classical Anglican statements:

'A Fruitful Exhortation to the Reading and Knowledge of Holy Scripture' in *The Homilies*, Book I (1547); 'An Information for them which take Offence at certain places of the Holy Scripture' in *The Homilies*, Book II (1571).

Thomas Cranmer: 'A Prologue or Preface . . . (to the Bible)' (1540) in *Remains and Letters* (Parker Society: Cambridge, 1846), pp. 118–125.

William Goode, *The Divine Rule of Faith and Practice*, especially Chapter XI, 'The Doctrine of the Church of England and her principal Divines on the subject of this work' (London, 2 vols., 1842).

Richard Hooker: *Laws of Ecclesiastical Polity*, especially Books I. xiii–xxiv, V. xx–xxii (I–IV, 1594; V, 1597). Several editions printed in the last century at Oxford.

John Jewel: *A Treatise of the Holy Scriptures* (preached, 1570; printed, 1582) in *Works* (Parker Society: Cambridge, 1850), Vol. IV, pp. 1161–1188.

William Whitaker: *A Disputation on Holy Scripture against the Papists* (1588) (Parker Society: Cambridge, 1849).

Compare also:

John Calvin: *Institutes of the Christian Religion*, especially Books I. vi–x, IV. viii–ix (1559; English translations available by H. Beveridge and J. T. McNeill).

George H. Tavard: *Holy Writ or Holy Church* (London, 1959). A Roman discussion applauding some Caroline divines.

(*b*) Modern views:

(i) Surveys:

Raymond Abba: *The Nature and Authority of the Bible* (London, 1958).

John Baillie: *The Idea of Revelation in Recent Thought* (Oxford, 1956).

ed. J. Baillie and H. Martin: *Revelation* (London, 1938).

H. D. McDonald: *Ideas of Revelation, an historical study 1700–1860* (London, 1959); *Theories of Revelation, an historical study 1860–1960* (London, 1963).

A. Richardson: *The Bible in the Age of Science* (London, 1961).

(ii) Individual statements:

Karl Barth: *Church Dogmatics* I/1, I/2, 'The Doctrine of the Word of God' (Edinburgh, 1936, 1956). See also K. Runia: *Karl Barth's Doctrine of Holy Scripture* (Grand Rapids, 1962).

Emil Brunner: *Revelation and Reason* (London, 1947). See also P. K. Jewett: *Emil Brunner's Concept of Revelation* (London, 1954).

Rudolf Bultmann: 'The Concept of Revelation in the New Testament' in *Existence and Faith* (writings by Bultmann, selected, translated, and introduced by S. M. Ogden) (London, 1961), pp. 58–91.

C. H. Dodd: *The Authority of the Bible* (London, 1929, 1960). Liberal Protestant.

C. Gore: *The Holy Spirit and the Church* (London, 1924). Liberal catholic.

Gabriel Hebert: *The Authority of the Old Testament* (London, 1947); *The Bible from Within* (Oxford, 1950) The 'biblical theology' approach.

(c) Revelation and Inspiration:

G. C. Berkouwer: *General Revelation* (Grand Rapids, 1955).
ed. C. F. H. Henry: *Revelation and the Bible* (London, 1959).
A. Kuyper: *Principles of Sacred Theology* (Grand Rapids, 1954). A work of genius.
J. Orr: *Revelation and Inspiration* (London, 1910).
H. Wheeler Robinson: *Inspiration and Revelation in the Old Testament* (Oxford, 1946).
B. B. Warfield: *The Inspiration and Authority of the Bible* (London, 1951).
E. J. Young: *Thy Word is Truth* (London, 1963).

(d) Biblical Authority:

N. Geldenhuys: *Supreme Authority* (London, 1953).
J. I. Packer: '*Fundamentalism*' *and the Word of God* (London, 1958).
B. Ramm: *The Witness of the Spirit* (Grand Rapids, 1959).
Works by Warfield, Kuyper, Hooker, Goode, as cited above.